Yes, God!

"Do you ever wonder about those miraculous parenting secrets that yield vocations to the priesthood and religious life, or simply lead to faith-filled families? In *Yes, God!* Susie Lloyd shares compelling stories of those who have opened their hearts and their lives to God's will, and offers a look into the homes that formed these generous souls. Compelling, lively, and filled with life lessons for any person of faith."

Lisa M. Hendey

Author of *A Book of Saints for Catholic Moms*

"*Yes, God!* is an interesting book that offers readers a rare chance to know some remarkable families of priests and religious sisters. Whether or not they are Catholic, everybody loves to talk about priests and nuns—theirs is an utterly fascinating life choice. I am fascinated by Susie Lloyd's own experiences of raising and homeschooling seven children. No matter where you are on your Catholic journey, you can't help but come away from this book humbled and inspired about what it means to be a parent. Lloyd does not preach. She tells beautiful stories full of humor and heartfelt introspection. You feel that Lloyd cares so much about raising kids to have faith—and her care rubs off."

Elizabeth Kuhns Douglas

Author of *The Habit: A History of the Clothing of Catholic Nuns*

Yes, God!

What Ordinary Families
Can Learn about Parenting
from Today's Vocation
Stories

SUSIE LLOYD

ave maria press AMP notre dame, indiana

© 2013 by Susan Lloyd

Founded in 1865, Ave Maria Press is a ministry of the United States Province of Holy Cross.

www.avemariapress.com

Paperback: ISBN-10 1-59471-406-1, ISBN-13 978-1-59471-406-1

E-book: ISBN-10 1-59471-407-X, ISBN-13 978-1-59471-407-8

Cover image © Thinkstock.com

Cover design by Andrew Wagoner.

Text design by Katherine Robinson.

Printed and bound in the United States of America.

Library of Congress Cataloging-in-Publication Data is available.

In thanks to God
for great parents.
I have no excuses.

The Rich
Young Man

As [Jesus] was setting out on a journey, a man ran up, knelt down before him, and asked him, "Good teacher, what must I do to inherit eternal life?"

Jesus answered him, "Why do you call me good? No one is good but God alone. You know the commandments: 'You shall not kill; you shall not commit adultery; you shall not steal; you shall not bear false witness; you shall not defraud; honor your father and your mother.'"

He replied and said to him, "Teacher, all of these I have observed from my youth."

Jesus, looking at him, loved him and said to him, "You are lacking in one thing. Go, sell what you have, and give to [the] poor and you will have treasure in heaven; then come, follow me."

At that statement his face fell, and he went away sad, for he had many possessions.

—Mark 10:17–22

Contents

Foreword

Human life is a journey. Towards what destination?
How do we find the way? Life is like a voyage on
the sea of history, often dark and stormy, a voyage in
which we watch for the stars that indicate the route.
The true stars of our life are the people who have
lived good lives. They are lights of hope. Certainly,
Jesus Christ is the true light, the sun that has risen
above all the shadows of history. But to reach him
we also need lights close by—people who shine with
his light and so guide us along our way.

—*Spe Salvi*, 49

Pope Emeritus Benedict XVI wrote in *Spe Salvi* that we
need help in navigating the voyage of life. We look to the
stars of our life to guide us: "The true stars of our life are
the people who have lived good lives. They are lights of
hope." Of course, we have Mary and the saints. But we
also need nearby stars: our friends, our parents, wise folk
who have gone the journey a little ahead of us, and so can
light the path for us.

In a culture that is often dark and discouraging, who
are the stars that guide our way as parents? Once upon a
time, we gathered around the kitchen table, while grandmothers, great-aunts, friends and neighbors would share
their stories and their wisdom. Extended families, where
we learn from the wisdom of parents and grandparents,
are rare these days.

Susie Lloyd and her latest book *Yes, God!* is a star that guides us.

Reading this book is like sitting across the table with Susie; we are sipping our coffee in a cluttered but homey kitchen, chatting about parenting. Susie shares her own (often humorous) parenting tales, and we talk about the inspiration she found while interviewing ten consecrated men and women—priests, nuns, and sisters from a variety of orders—for her latest book.

We parents tend to get intimidated by "perfect" families (the ones whose nine chapel-veiled children are lined up in the front pew at daily Mass). Or the saints and martyrs. How can we ever hope to live up to these ideals?

It's not that we want to make sure we have at least one priest and one nun in every family, but rather, we want our children to be faithful, to be heroic, to be open to God's will. Or at least, as Susie says, we don't want to "blow it" as parents. And that is what this book is about. Five priests, five nuns, and the parents who raised them to say "yes" to God.

In this book of stories about parents who have raised heroic kids, kids open to God's call, we find guiding wisdom. Susie brings us together to hear about some of their joys and setbacks, to discover their guiding principles and rallying cries, to pass along tips from the "master" parents.

Susie gives us hope. She tells us about Sister Marie José de la Rosa's parents, whose parents persevered in marriage despite disability and poverty. She relates how the parents of Sister Chiara Marie and Sister Marie St. Francis broke the cycle of abuse and alcoholism in their family ancestry. And then there is blind Father Ezaki, whose dad was a Buddhist.

These are ordinary folks like you and me, striving to raise their children well, struggling with the same daily trials: finances, physical disability, emotional trauma, wayward kids, an aggressive culture. Some of the families are large, others small. Some were homeschooled and others went to public school. Interspersed throughout are humorous and poignant anecdotes from Susie's own family life.

It is rare to find extended families these days, or even communities of faith where the older parents share with the younger practical wisdom and memories of their own childhoods. Susie brings us together to hear the stories and to discover the wisdom, to pass along the tips from the "master" parents . . . just as we might have done a few generations ago, learning from grandmothers and mothers, talking over the fence or sharing a cup of coffee at the kitchen table.

We find a few more guiding stars shining in the dark night, and we come away from reading *Yes, God!* filled with laughter and hope.

Art and Laraine Bennett
Authors of *The Temperament God Gave You*

Introduction

Once a week, my husband, Greg, and I would pile our seven kids into our rickety van and drive up the hill to choir practice. It was held in a stately, stone edifice that was, in its halcyon days, a seminary. The finely chiseled statues, the carved, honey woodwork, and the canopy-topped high altar were solidly built to last for centuries.

A mere eighty years after the seminary was built this extraordinary place was used as an ordinary retreat center. It was managed by our friend and choir director, Mike. It was there that five ordinary families—with varying talents but lots of passion, cheered on by extremely forgiving acoustics—learned to render the soaring Palestrina:

> *Sicut cervus desiderat ad fontes aquarum, ita desiderat anima mea ad te Deus.*

> *As the deer thirsts for springs of water, so my soul longs for you, O God.*

As we practiced, the voices of our younger children running around the halls outside the chapel made the place come alive. Their motto, "Make a joyful noise," helped make up for the empty, former-seminary feel of the place.

If you stood in the long, grand corridor and listened, you could almost hear the ghostly echoes of young men's feet long ago, the bouncing of basketballs down in the gym, the seminarians' laughter, the clink of cutlery against dinner plates, and the solemn chanting of the nightly office.

It was there that this book began.

In 2008, a shy seminarian on retreat chanced to hear us sing. Joseph Eddy quietly approached Mike and asked if we would sing at his ordination to the Mercedarian Order.

Wait. *The who?* Despite being a cradle Catholic, long used to all that is strange and offbeat about my religion, I had never heard of this order. It was founded in 1218 by St. Peter Nolasco, under the direct request of Our Lady. Its members would give their lives as ransom for Christians who were captives of the Moors.

His invitation made my year. I was sure my mom had arranged the whole thing from her perch in heaven. Priests were her favorite thing. Her favorite saint was the Curé of Ars, whose daily potato she would have dearly loved to boil. My getting an ordination gig was . . . well, it was like karma.

It wasn't until the day Joseph Eddy became an *alter Christus* (another Christ) that I actually got a good look at this shy, new priest. At first, I saw only the back of his head as he lay face down on the stone floor in St. Ann's Basilica in Scranton, Pennsylvania. For him, since he was so shy, it was probably the most comfortable moment of the day—much better than the plush, air-conditioned, catered reception that would follow, with its mandatory speech making.

Eventually, when he bobbed back up, I was astonished. At thirty-one, with fair hair and boyish looks, he seemed to me like someone who'd say, "Dad, can I borrow the car to get to ordination?" I resisted the urge to nudge my fellow choir members and whisper, "Who is this kid?" There was something captivating and hopeful about his youth and his vitality. He could have been anything he wanted, and yet he had chosen the priesthood.

It suddenly didn't matter that he was the only one being ordained that day—that he was but a drop in a dried-up river of vocations—that the times were against him and his kind. *He made it!* A mere drop, yes, but that drop was another Christ, and for me it signaled the turning of the tide.

The whole choir felt it. Our voices chimed and rang like caroling bells as we sang,

Tu es sacerdos in aeternum!

You are a priest forever!

At the reception, I stole glances at his parents. Did I detect the faint outline of a halo hovering around their heads? Nope. They seemed like ordinary Americans, like me. I became aware of an embarrassing desire to pump them for information about how to raise children.

After that day, whenever I would meet a lively young priest or a pretty young sister, I would wonder—and sometimes ask—what their homes were like. It's not that I wanted to get one of our children to become a priest or a nun; that's God's call. I just wanted to raise faithful kids. All right, I'll go further: I wanted to raise heroic kids—kids who could say yes to God in whatever way he calls.

Or at least, I didn't want to blow it.

Slowly, the concept for this book took shape. It's my first and probably my last attempt at a "parenting" book. Not your standard how-to (be-like-me) book, it is filled with stories of people who are wiser than I. They have allowed me—and now you—into their homes, like friends. Isn't that the way most of us learn how to live?

Didn't the apostle Philip tell Nathanael about Jesus with the words, "Come and see?"

You may be wondering: Who are these kids? None of them are famous so why should you care about them?" Each of the ten priests, nuns, and sisters in this book represents, for me, a modern-day "rich young man." As Americans, they possessed more than the rich young man of the gospel could have dreamed possible, not just in material conveniences, but also in education, freedom, and opportunity.

Like the rest of us, they grew up in a culture surrounded by a host of evils—selfishness, indifference to God and neighbor, loss of the sense of the sacred—yet they overcame them. Why? Something was right about their homes that prepared them not only to reject evil but also to embrace a heroic life.

They come from varied backgrounds—some from large families, some from small. Some of their moms worked outside the home; some stayed home and homeschooled. Some of their dads were devout Catholics; some were not. Some of their parents came from happy homes and some from quite the opposite.

Yet there is one common thread that binds all of them together and that is precisely the reason I as a parent care about them—and why you should too. Not one of them went away sad.

From Ordinary to
Extraordinary

Saying Yes to Duty

Father Joseph Eddy, O. de M.

> **I wanted to be special at something.**

Father Joseph Eddy is not from any of the places I expected.

He's not from a jumbo-sized family. In fact, he is the youngest of three, and his parents, Thomas and Mary, were rather surprised by his arrival. They called him the "bonus baby." Mrs. Eddy had so much trouble delivering

1

his two sisters that doctors said it was dangerous for her
to have any more. Thus, as Joseph came into the world,
his parish priest was already offering Mass for his life and
that of his mom.

Young Joe wasn't homeschooled. He wasn't educated
at a specialized academy run by high-minded, counter-
cultural laymen or religious. He didn't go to a parochial
school. His parents sent him to the only school in town,
which was public. He didn't attend any of the small
mega-Catholic colleges, such as Franciscan University of
Steubenville, where students major in theology and minor
in matrimony or Holy Orders. He didn't grow up with
the Latin Mass. And I'm willing to bet his home wasn't
decorated to look like a shrine.

He and I do have one thing in common though: a
devotion to St. Joseph. His beats mine. It goes back to
before he was born and is, in fact, how he got his name.

Joseph Eddy was the child of a promise. After his parents were married, Mr. Eddy had difficulty finding work.
He is a disabled Vietnam veteran, shot in his left arm—
mere inches from his heart. So, Joe's mom enrolled her
husband in the St. Joseph Union, which promised prayers
to help him find a job. In two weeks he had three offers.
He took one as a technician at IBM. Thus, St. Joseph, the
patron of workers and the patron of fathers, became the
patron of the Eddys' only son.

Of course, most Catholics have a devotion to St.
Joseph's better half. Father Joseph recalls, "We had a large
statue of Our Lady of Grace in our home. As a child, I
would look at her and recognize Mary as another Mother
who was assigned to take care of me."

Neighbors didn't need to tour the statuary to notice
that the Eddys were not Baptist like most of their

neighbors. A simple recitation of the family litany would do: Thomas, Mary, Maria, Teresa, and Joseph.

They maintained a close relationship with the parish, which, thanks to an old-fashioned pastor, might as well have been called St. Smells and Bells. Young Joe spent a lot of time with this quiet, sober man since Joe's great-aunt ran the rectory. She was one of those formidable great-aunts that make standard-issue aunts look harmless and doddering. Together, she and Father Antediluvian were not a lot of fun, but their sobriety made for a solid parish.

So far everything about the Eddys seems to have been plainer than parsnips. Or was it? To understand the depth of their native Catholicism, you have to go back another generation to the families of Mary and Thomas.

Mary was born into a family of farmers. Her parents were in their forties when she was born. She was an only child. As if farmers weren't a down-to-earth lot already, Mary's folks grew up with the shortages of the Depression and World War II. In those hard times, farmers marked their fences so that hoboes knew where they could get a hot meal and a night's rest. Mary's family still kept the fence marked well after the war. Men often got off the train, did some work on the farm, ate, rested, and were off again the next day. Mary grew up simply, with no pretensions. Her folks' idea of a good time involved visiting neighboring relatives for a chat. Father Joseph recalls his grandparents as people who would do anything to help anyone.

Mary raised her children the same way, even though the circumstances were quite different. Joseph grew up in the prosperous 1980s in a comfortable, new housing development. Behind it was a trailer park full of poor families.

"Mom would drag us to the neighbors' houses often," says Father Joseph. She made Joe and his sisters help the neighbors shovel snow or cut their grass. "One old woman had dementia, and one old man was kind of nasty. But there we were, the three children, doing chores for them. Of course, we complained. But Mom just insisted that it was the right thing to do."

St. Francis de Sales tells us that those who are rich can practice poverty just the way Mrs. Eddy did:

> The servant is less than the master; therefore make yourself a servant of the poor. Go and wait on them when they are sick in bed, wait on them, I say, with your own hands. Prepare their food for them your-self and at your own expense. Be their seamstress and laundress. Philothea, such service is more glo-rious than that of a king. (*Introduction to the Devout Life*)

Such was the unassuming Mrs. Eddy. She was a farm girl who loved homespun wisdom ("You've gotta kiss a lot of frogs before you find your prince") and backwoods sayings ("I haven't seen you in a coon's age!"). "It embar-rassed us," says Father Joseph. (Hey, what are parents for?) "But we always knew she was the real deal. What you see is what you get."

Joe's father, Thomas, brought something very different to the family. Some would call it "baggage." He is intro-spective and quiet—not without cause. His childhood had not been peaceful. Grandpa Eddy was aggressive and sometimes violent. Grandma Eddy was passive aggres-sive. But Grandma, for all her controlling ways, was Cath-olic. She faithfully took her children to Mass.

Go ahead. Go ahead and say it: "If her religion doesn't make her a nice person, it's a failure." That's what people always say.

I prefer to look at it the way Evelyn Waugh, the author of *Brideshead Revisited*, did: "You have no idea how much nastier I would be if I was not a Catholic." That was Grandma. It was no small grace that she was steadfast in the Faith. Such perseverance does not go unrewarded. As she lay dying, her future-priest grandson prayed the Chaplet of Divine Mercy at her bedside.

Perhaps an even greater victory was when Grandpa, an unchurched Baptist all his life, became a Catholic. He then prepared for his death with frequent confession. If the heavens are moved at the conversion of this one sinner, imagine what hope it instilled in Thomas and his family.

As Mrs. Eddy brought heroic generosity into her marriage, Mr. Eddy brought heroic suffering. His heart was formed in silence. Father Joseph says that his father isn't one to speak of his pain, which is perhaps typical of previous generations when men did not cry. He isn't one to speak of his accomplishments, though, either, as men across the generations love to do. Perhaps it's something left over from boyhood. Whenever I hear a grown man get excited and announce an achievement, it reminds me of an exchange I once heard between two homeschooled boys:

"I read *The Three Musketeers*—unabridged."

"Oh, yeah? Well, I read it in *French*."

Kids oppressed by angry households tend to go the other way. They do not seek attention. It's safer to be invisible.

I once wrote a story about a recovering alcoholic named Jerry, whose father was an angry alcoholic. He described his childhood living with this man: "If you got hurt and cried or were having a good time and laughed, he got angry and you got beat." Jerry stayed safe by not showing any emotions. "You learn to turn off your emotions. You do not know how to turn them on."

Father Joseph confesses being ashamed that it took so many years, into his young adulthood, for him to appreciate his unassuming father. "Dad was a man of fidelity, a quiet leader, a great provider, and a good protector. I imagine that St. Joseph was a quiet man who just did his thing."

Who just did his thing—take a look around, and you'll see how big this really is. Many men today do not know the meaning of the word "sacrifice." They seek only to be pleased. As Jerry's own battle against anger and alcoholism shows, those from abusive homes often become abusive. Down the line it goes, from generation to generation. Only the bravest of them stop the cycle. Joe's dad was that man.

"Dad was not perfect, he had a temper, but he always asked for forgiveness, and I always remember him getting into his truck on Saturdays and going alone to confession." Only the humblest of them repent. Joe's dad was that man.

No doubt, the Eddys think they are ordinary Americans. Nothing special. In their house, grace was found through ordinary means: the sacraments, the Rosary. Yet, "ordinary" does not mean "nothing special." It means that these are the channels of grace the Church recommends for all Christians.

Like their neighbors, the Eddys pursued the American Dream. They wanted to give their kids everything they didn't have. They raised their family in the era when more and more women were working outside the home, not from necessity, but for personal satisfaction. Mrs. Eddy, who was a trained teacher, was right there with them. Yet, there were periods, a year or two at a time, when she decided the job just wasn't worth it—when it was wearing her out or when it seemed that the kids needed more of her. Family always came first.

To counteract the culture of materialism, Joe and his sisters were expected to get jobs when they were twelve. Designer clothes were in—but if Joe wanted them he would have to spend his own money on them. He did that—once.

It was a good lesson to adjust his desires to fit his budget. More importantly, he learned to build an identity based on more than appearances. Like most kids, it was a lesson he didn't want to learn. "As I got into junior high and high school, I felt a bit lost. My friends were changing and I didn't fit in with anyone. I felt plain and was embarrassed by my quiet family." So he set out to build an identity based on achievement.

"I wanted to be special at something. I was average at sports, had average looks, and was an average student. I wanted to show everyone that I was more than average, that I could be special. I began to focus intensely on being perfect. I would outwork everyone in sports, school, and whatever else."

Joe's family wasn't sure what to make of this. Who wouldn't want an achiever for a son? On the other hand, the kid was driving himself nuts.

It reminds me of the story of Venerable Walter Ciszek, S.J. As a young seminarian, he competed with himself to

be tougher than he already was—swimming in icy water,
fasting on bread and water during Lent, suffering self-
imposed loneliness, all just to see if he could take it. It was
part of his preparation to be a priest who would spend
twenty-three years behind the Iron Curtain, most of them
in the gulag of Siberia. Great—except he didn't have his
superior's permission for any of it. His headstrong ways
almost got him kicked out of the Jesuit novitiate. What
God really wanted from him was obedience—the tough-
est thing of all.

Joe's superiors found him stubborn, too. "Mom, Dad,
and Grandma tried to talk to me about it, but they had
little effect on my strong disposition. I think it was my
grandmother's prayers (a Rosary for each grandchild)
that eventually got me out of my destructive mindset."

As Providence would have it, Joe's dad was there for
him at this turning point in his life. Thomas's latest cross
was losing his job of twenty-one years. Since he was close
to earning his retirement, his job was cut first. This was a
crushing blow to his identity as provider. But God wanted
him to provide for his family in a different way—by being
more present to his children. Joe wasn't the only one who
needed him especially at that time. "My sisters were rebel-
lious," he recalls. "My dad became more involved in the
parenting then, and they responded to him."

This trial by fire also allowed Thomas to finally open
himself up emotionally and show his human love for his
family. Joe used to think his father wasn't affectionate. He
admits his concept of affection was conditioned by the
emotive trends on TV and in school. "Dad would show
affection to my sisters with hugs, but it was different with
me. He would shake my hand, and we would see who

had a stronger grip, or we would wrestle—that is, until I accidentally broke his ribs."

Everyone in Joe's family now sees the layoff as a blessing in disguise. "We finally got the father that we needed."

Joe also joined a Protestant youth group and met Christian friends, such as Dan, whose dad was an evangelical pastor. Wait a minute. A red flag just went straight up the pole and is flapping in a high wind. As a homeschooler, I know what these folks are like. They are friendly and respectful and highly unlikely to sneak your teenager out of the house for a midnight drinking binge. They may, however, try to argue him straight out of the Catholic Church. Dan was all of the above. Joe's mom allowed the kids to belong to the youth group but warned them against being recruited.

Joe took the good he saw in Dan and made it his own. Dan never used bad language; he was never cruel; he was genuine and unashamed of being Christian. Best of all, Dan's zeal to convert Joe backfired. "He challenged me. We had many discussions and arguments about the Catholic Church and what Christianity is." This spurred Joe to start studying his faith more. The friendship was just what Joe needed to emerge as the leader he was born to be.

Still, the thought of doing anything as public as being a priest terrified him. "I was so deathly shy about public speaking or even public walking!" His high school class of 130 students voted him "Most Shy Male." Apparently, Divine Providence enjoys a challenge.

Father Joseph recalls, "One day after serving Mass, a well-respected man from the parish came up to me and told me that God spoke to him at Mass. God told him that

I was called to become a priest. To me this was amazing, because I thought that there were many better candidates among the altar servers. I was the shy, nervous one. Why would God choose me?"

Perhaps good St. Joseph once asked himself the same question. A famously quiet, dutiful soul, he probably felt he was nobody special. If there had been a village year-book, he would have been voted "Most Unlikely to Make Sudden Epic Journeys." Yet, it was just this plainness, this stability, really, that God wanted for his service. As patron saints go, how spot-on can you get?

I am convinced that God is a fan of dutiful ordinariness. He uses it to do miracles. How else could an amateur, family choir such as ours render the soaring Palestrina? How else could a plain-as-parsnips family give a son to the sacred priesthood? How else could we and they—strangers from different worlds—come together to celebrate that sacred day as members of one and the same Church?

Saying Yes to Duty

I arrived on the motherhood scene with zip experience. My list of previous engagements read:

- No younger siblings.

- One summer in role of warm body, aka babysitter. Job description: eating in front of reruns, hoping kids are not drowning in pool. (What did they expect for a dollar an hour?)

- Cameo appearance as teenage aunt—playing opposite niece and nephew who knock on bedroom door to play at 9 a.m. before I am up. Response: turn Walkman up higher.

- Part ownership of world's most-obedient Labrador retriever.

Kids, who know an amateur when they see one, generally left me alone. This was fine with me since when they weren't leaving me alone, they usually wanted a piece of what I was eating.

If I hadn't been Catholic, I probably would have avoided children all together, convinced that I'd make a terrible mother. But, on our wedding day, Greg and I had vowed "to accept children lovingly from God." It was our duty. Nine months and one week after the wedding, our duty was born. We named her Kate.

Help!

So I asked my brother Dan for advice. He had trained Grigio, the world's most obedient Labrador retriever, and as far as I could tell was having similar results with his small son. Could he tell me, please, what to do?

He shrugged and said simply, "We just spend a lot of time with him."

I didn't expect it to be so easy. You mean all you have to do is show up? Even I can do that.

Time. I had plenty of it. I was home all day. What else would I do, other than spend time with the kid? Lock myself in the bathroom?

I didn't realize that it would be hard.

For me, it meant my list of personal interests shrank to things that involved craft paper and glue. It meant becoming a lifetime member of the *Little House on the Prairie* rerun club. It meant peanut-butter-and-graham-cracker lunches because restocking the pantry meant going out with all of the kids, having to climb the seats—often in an advanced state of pregnancy—to buckle and unbuckle. I had a friend who just threw the kids loosely into the car and ignored the flailing arms and legs in the rearview mirror, which was the way of our mothers' generation, but I couldn't.

But that wasn't so bad. The hard part was the self-doubt. Being a homemaker was not "in." What if people thought I wasn't brave enough or smart enough to do anything but stay home? What if they were right?

Yet when I thought of where I was needed most, there was only one answer. Home.

Doing my daily duty, putting in the time, slowly changed me from the person who turned the Walkman up higher to the person who gets out of bed at 4 a.m. to clean up barf.

A mom once said to me that after you have kids you can still live your life just as you did before. "Life goes on," she said. Does it? I don't think so. What actually happens is that a little part of you dies—namely, the part that always got to do whatever it wanted.

No one can doubt that Mrs. Eddy was brave enough and smart enough to work outside the home while raising her family. Yet, she gave it up—as we must all be ready to give up good things for better things—when her family needed more of her. Even when she did charity work, she understood the balance of her duties. She did not trek to the soup kitchen across town. She just went next door.

When Mr. Eddy lost his job of more than twenty years, a part of his self-worth died. Yet, it coincided with a time in the kids' teenage development that called for the strong, protective arm of a father. And he was there.

People are afraid of having children. They sense that they will lose a little bit of themselves. They are right. But when that little part of you dies, you become free from it so that you, a better you, can rise in a way you didn't plan but that God had waiting for you.

Team
Spirit

Saying Yes to Affection

Sister Brigid Mary Rock, I.H.M.

It was Rock versus whoever would dare show up.

The brown, needle-covered path was blessedly shady and cool. I had just stepped off the hot, open field at Morning Star Camp in New England. Nicknamed "Nun Camp," Morning Star is run by the Slaves of the Immaculate Heart of Mary in Still River, Massachusetts. Parents like me were arriving to pick up their daughters.

Moments before, our oldest had run up to me and exclaimed, "Oh, Mom, you have to meet these *awesome nuns*! If I ever become a nun, I want to be one of them!" This, coming from Miss I'll-Never-Be-a-Nun, was impressive.

For one week, the campers had lived in another world—one that I know only from old books—a world benevolently presided over by youthful sisters in sweeping habits. As I watched, a few of these walked serenely across the dazzling field—as if the searing heat itself dared not touch the black cloth of their habits.

They were the real light of this place, I mused—a gentle, dappled light like the one filtering through the pines.

"You can't hit the broad side of a barn!" The cry rent the air in front of me. I stepped into the open to see one of the sisters armed with bow and arrow, teaching some girls archery—in vain, apparently. Dressed to the nines in black-and-white formal wear, she evoked "the Penguin" from the Blues Brothers. Don't mess with her. Thus went my first encounter with Sister Brigid Mary—while she was yelling at my children. Ah, a kindred spirit.

Would you believe the girls were eating it up?

They tell me that she's "the funny sister," the one most likely to bluntly tell them the embarrassing truth about themselves without any trace of rancor—and then jump gamely into a boat to take them sailing.

"She's the one," they tell me, "who really doesn't fit the mold."

∗

Sister Brigid was born grabbing life by the horns— literally. Rebecca (Sister Brigid's given name) or Bec, as her family called her, was the seventh of Grace and James Rock's nine kids brought up on a Vermont dairy farm.

Farming is a time-consuming occupation that does not permit, say, also working full-time for IBM. That's true for most of us, anyway. Sister's dad, James Rock, did both and still managed to win awards and a couple of patents. After he got home from work, he would put in the rest of his fifteen-hour day on the farm. Wait, did I just use the word "rest"?

Now, I've always been proud—to the point of bragging—of my engineer dad who bought land and grew crops when I was a kid. Our farm, however, was only a weekend gig. We stuck to raising things that could be left alone most of the time, such as carrots. We didn't even have a self-sufficient farm cat. The Rocks had thirty head of cattle, each weighing in at half a ton, plus whatever else is usually found on Old MacDonald's farm.

Sister rates the whole experience as fun, even the pigs and the unending work. This was the moment in my interview with her when I realized that I am out of her league.

The fact that it was fun had a lot to do with her dad. Sister says his peacefulness permeated everything. The kids saw it in little things, such as the way he did the haying with a Rosary in his hand. Even the cows felt it. When one of the new cows thrashed, he controlled the animal by praying Hail Marys aloud to her until she calmed down. "It was like Superman praying the Rosary," Sister says.

Actually, he sounds more like the Incredible Hulk. "He was huge." Yet, she says with some reservation, he was not like some Catholic dads she's seen who are "aggressively domineering" to their wives and kids, who

think it's their God-given right and duty to make everybody miserable.

Mr. Rock's gentleness did more to create family har-
mony than authoritarianism ever could. "My parents
had an unbreakable unity. They argued sometimes, but
it never got ugly. They never let resentment build." Sister
says that each did what was necessary, regardless of self.
They were a team.

Mom and Dad played sports with their kids. Mom
wowed them with her basketball skills, and Dad played
football. Sister told me about their annual Thanksgiving
Day Turkey Bowl. "It was Rock versus whoever would
dare show up. My brother would invite his friends.
They'd play us *once*. We'd slaughter them."

So, did any of the kids ever test the unity within the
family by, say, going to one parent for a yes when the
other had already said no? Sister Brigid answers, "I tried
it *once*. We all tried it once." This never works when you
have a pile of siblings. There are narcs everywhere. In
fact, you're lucky if all they do is tell on you, rather than
torture and kill you themselves. Pitting Mom and Dad
against each other is a capital crime.

Growing up with so many siblings, Sister Brigid adds,
was good preparation for convent life. "When you live
in close quarters with a houseful of women who aren't
related to you, you have to work things out. You can't be
contentious. You learn to sacrifice. You can't have tiny
gripes. If one person is selfish, it affects the whole community." She tells me that working things out is something her parents taught them, mainly by staying out of
the kids' squabbles. People with nine kids and a farm
to manage don't have time to meddle in every quarrel.

When they do, you know it's big, and it gets everyone's attention.

Once, one of Sister's siblings strayed away from the Faith. "She was making all these stupid decisions. The rest of us wanted to kill her," she says. "We're Irish. If we're not fighting a common enemy, we're fighting each other." Mom surprised them all by coming to her wayward child's defense. Sister Brigid says of her mom, "She told us we were not perfect either. First and foremost, she is our sister and we're responsible for her salvation." And the daughter? "Then she told my sister she had to stop it."

Grace Rock took the focus off fighting each other and put it back on fighting the common enemy: Satan. Like her namesake, Our Lady of Grace, her arms were open wide to her children as she planted her heel squarely on the head of the serpent—and drew her child back into the fold.

Real contention of this sort was rare. Mom and Dad didn't have to strong-arm the kids into obedience. The name Rock suits them. They were a fortress.

So it's a wonder to me that Bec decided to ram up against this fortress when she was fifteen. She got up late one Sunday and announced that she didn't feel like going to Mass. Mrs. Rock turned to Mr. Rock and said, "Jim, what do you think of that?" He looked up from his paper and asked, "How do you want to spend eternity?" and went back to his paper.

She went to Mass.

I know there's a lesson here about how staying calm and cool is more effective than shouting and lecturing. You get that. But I'm more interested in how stupid fifteen-year-olds are. *Let's see. I'm too tired to ride in the back of the car to go to Mass. I know! I'll pick a fight with Dad—who wrangles steers—and Mom—who can slam dunk me through the hoop in the back yard.*

This is important because half the battle of raising kids is expecting them to be stupid now and then. Did you notice how Mr. and Mrs. Rock didn't bother with the martyr routine? They just looked her in the eye and let her know what was at stake—her salvation. No rants about their authority were used or needed. That was how they taught the Faith and all the details that came with it.

There is a saying that the Faith is better caught than taught. The main condition for catching the Faith is a happy home. If nothing but strictness rules, the kids look for a way out.

Instead, people outside the family were looking for a way in. "My mom was loved by everybody. Friends came and went constantly. *Normal* friends," she stresses. So this wasn't an enclave of Catholic weirdness? It wasn't a family of apparition-chasing, rapture-talking, chastisement hopefuls? The Rocks' farm was a place where Catholics and non-Catholics gathered to have good times. The Faith was there as something natural, easy, and happy. People were attracted to it, such as one of the boys' coaches who was a "fall-away" Catholic. Sister's brother brought him back to the Church.

This was how it felt to be inside the family, even as a guest. You were part of a tight community. If you were outside of it, you didn't want to go up against it.

You think they were dangerous at the Turkey Bowl? Try telling Mrs. Rock you owned her children. That's exactly what the principal of their school did. Mrs. Rock was constantly battling for her children's right to a decent education. Sex-ed had just come to the public high school and was threatening to seep, like grimy water, into the lower grades. When Mrs. Rock complained, the principal told her, "Once those kids pass through the door, they're mine."

Really, you almost feel sorry for him.

"Every month she was down at the statehouse. She went to teachers' meetings, too. Everybody dreaded when my mother walked through the door."

When Grace finally decided that it would be easier to homeschool the last four kids, the schools probably threw her a going-away party. "They were relieved," says Sister Brigid.

Now you know where Sister gets her "Don't mess with me" attitude. So I ask her, was it difficult for someone with such a strong will to submit to convent life? "The hardest thing in religious life is learning to submit to superiors who are not your parents," she admits. "You mean, like, what if they stick you with a name like Hiltrudis?" I suggest.

She assures me that even under such conditions, the grace of the vocation is there.

As spirited as she is, Sister Brigid was trained by her mom and dad in obedience as well as spunk. To my girls she may not look as if she fits in with the rest of the religious sisters, but she is exactly the type the sisters want playing on their team.

Sister describes the moment in her mid-twenties when her dad walked her down the aisle. He was delivering her as a bride in a white gown to Christ and also as a sister to a new family. It was a new domestic Church, one she had prepared for all her life. She talks in fragments as if such a moment is hard to express. "Growing up, you dream of this moment, the perfect guy, the spectacular train. This is

more sublime. And the priest says that if you are faithful
to this, God promises you eternal life."

That is something married people need to learn, too.
If you are faithful to your vocation, God promises you
eternal life. The Rocks are seeing the fruits of *their* faith-
fulness: five children married, one daughter a religious
sister, twenty-four grandchildren, and nine out of nine
children who have embraced the Faith as their own.

The Rocks know what it feels like to be undefeated in
more ways than one. It isn't often that you hear of a large
Catholic family that can echo the words of Christ, "Father,
I've lost none of those you've given me."

Saying Yes to Affection

Mother Janet Erskine Stuart, the author of the 1911 book
The Education of Catholic Girls, says that the most important thing you can teach children is that God is a loving
Father. You do this first by showing your children that
you love them.

This is easy when they're babies. They're so cute that
you are drawn to them. They fit neatly on your lap. They
don't wreck your stuff and then shrug it off. Older kids,
on the other hand, can make you want to crouch behind
a wall, pounce out, and pound them into the carpet.

I used to think I was the only one who felt this way.
Then I started speaking at conferences, and moms would
come up to me and confide their guilt. Yes, guilt. Each felt
like she was the only unnatural mother in the Catholic
Church. Oh sure, the *real world* out there can't stand its
teenagers. But we Catholics, we're supposed to be above
that.

I tell them this story.

One day I went to see a saintly Italian priest, a Padre Pio knockoff. I wanted advice about an entirely different problem, but instead I poured out my feelings of bloodlust for my teenager. He listened patiently and without evident alarm.

Then slowly, in his rich Venetian accent, he asked, "Do you hug her?"

"Uh, no," I answered in my northeastern, nasal twang. "I'm trying to stay out of range."

"You have to show her you love her," he insisted.

"I do, Father! I take her to see her friends. I buy her the things she asks for—"

He interrupted me with a slight shake of his venerable, white head. "That is not the same thing. She needs to *feel* that you love her. *Phee-si-cally*. You have to *hug* her."

I could well have argued, "But Father, not everybody cares about physical affection. There are other love languages. In fact, some people just don't want to be touched." But I had come to him for his wisdom, since my own was a flop. He made me realize, with the words "You have to," that it really did not matter if I felt like hugging her or if she "deserved" it. It was my place to initiate affection, not hers, but mine. I was the parent.

Father himself showed me what to do. The next time he saw her, he gave her the kindest smile I have ever seen and held her hand for a moment. She responded to it as if she was having a vision of her guardian angel.

Following his simple advice changed everything for the better. I showed her that I loved her *phee-si-cally*, and she responded by becoming more lovable. We developed an open, confident relationship. I began thinking of her as cute—cute the way adolescents are, always trying to appear cool to hide their embarrassment.

I told this story to one lady, who lifted her eyes up to heaven (where the priest now resides). "Thank you, old Italian priest," she said.

Years later, I think often of this simple act. I consider how each of us comes dramatically, somewhat violently into the world and is immediately placed in the arms of our mothers and soothed. We are given back that physical sense of protection and warmth and belonging. I have since met souls who have confessed to me that their parents never hugged them and how deeply they missed it. One friend told me that she used to hope to get sick because once, when she was sick, her mom had pulled her onto her lap. Perhaps their parents could well have argued that they were showing love by providing, or paying for special lessons, or driving them to see their friends. Well and good. All I can say is that that's exactly how I had been showing love to my kid and it wasn't working. She needed a hug. Not just anybody's hug but my hug—the same hug that I had given her when she was born, with a worried look on her face, after hours of trying labor. They gave her into my arms and she immediately relaxed.

The Rocks got this right. Yes, they got a lot of things right—not much of which I am qualified to imitate. They are out of my league and so be it. Yet, I know that none of their superpowers would have meant a thing if they hadn't shown their kids how much they loved them—*phee-si-cally*. Dad lined the kids up every night and thumbed a cross on their foreheads and said, "God bless you and sleep well." To this day Mom visits the convent and kisses Sister Brigid Mary on the cheek, and Sister rubs the spot—not to rub it off but to rub it *in*. This is how those kids grew up knowing the love of God. This is how Sister is able to carry it to others.

Do you wish to see more light in the world? Then be a light bearer in your own home. Nothing sheds light in the world quite like a happy family. Let your home be like the Rocks' house where people walk in and experience Christian joy—where they can see exactly what those who knew the early Christians saw, "See how they love one another," and find themselves included in it. This is what our daughter was responding to when she ran up to me at camp that bright day exclaiming, "If I ever become a nun, I want to be one of them!"

This is every Christian's calling. It is how we participate locally in the grand conversion mission of the universal Church. I think of it every time I see a picture of Michelangelo's grand, arching colonnade leading to St. Peter's in Rome. The Church's arms are open wide, gathering us into her embrace.

A Holy
Boldness

Saying Yes to Strength

Father Joel Kiefer,
Diocese of Allentown, Pennsylvania

**My dad could beat up
the other dads.**

One mother I know thinks it's a bad sign when either your doctor or your priest is younger than you are. Years ago, when such a doctor joined our mutual ob-gyn practice, she declared, "I'm not going to him. He's a kid, and he has big hair." There's something to that. When it's time to entrust our bodies or souls to the care of another, youth does not inspire confidence. Neither does big hair.

Perhaps it is Father Joel Kiefer's West Point haircut that threw me off. I didn't realize that he's younger than I am. Or perhaps it's because I prefer to see my own reflection as St. Paul says, "through a glass darkly," the better to hide those little lines forming around my mouth. *O Mother of Perpetual Youth, pray for us.*

Perhaps it is something deeper that makes Father seem older than his years: a certain ease of office. You'd expect it from a guy coming out of the nation's top army institution, who then served six years culminating in the rank of captain. But it didn't start there. He learned it from his dad.

"My Father is a man's man, a big, barrel-chested German," he says with a hint of playground pride in his voice. For a moment, Father Kiefer, soldier, captain, and priest, disappears, and a ten-year-old Joel actually says to me, "My dad could beat up the other dads."

Would he? (I just have to ask.) Suddenly, Father Kiefer is back. "Oh, no. No, no, no, no, no."

"You're sure about that, Father?" I ask.

"Oh yes. He was the velvet hammer." He then launches into a story to clarify.

The scene: One hundred third-grade cub scouts in an auditorium. A sea wave of blue uniforms swelling, roaring, and crashing against each other. Mr. John Kiefer, scout leader, stepped up onto the stage, surveyed the mob, and silently raised his hand. There was instant order—like Christ calming the tempest.

The velvet hammer.

I get it. This is about the ability to command both respect and love—the mark of a leader.

Under such guidance, Father claims that his Bucks County, Pennsylvania, childhood was "perfect." I am surprised by this. Sure, home was great, but what about the rest of the world? This was the post–social revolution of the seventies and eighties. What was so perfect about it? In the seventies, streaking happened. Then came the eighties, which made up for the streaking by overdressing, with designer labels on the outside.

Then again . . . the neighborhoods were *alive* with kids. There were "fat kids, skinny kids, kids who climb on rocks," all playing together outside, Father Joel says. Yes, it was kind of perfect.

The boys shot hoops in the driveway every afternoon when John returned from work. He'd say, "Hi boys," and then go straight to their mom, Carol, to give her a kiss. Young Joel and his brother and sister felt secure knowing their dad and mom loved each other.

Most nights Dad tucked the kids into bed and talked to them, getting to know them, and allowing them to know him. "He opened our minds to the future, to our potential. He talked to us *older* than we were." He challenged all the kids never to be satisfied, always to reach higher. "I was probably the most motivated second grader in the history of Catholic education," says Father Joel.

That remains to this day in his parish work. "If I see nobody in line for confession, I am not satisfied. I begin thinking about what I can do to change that."

I saw this firsthand when I met Father Kiefer shortly after his ordination. He was based in a large, suburban parish. Its comfortable, middle-class population had a generous share of occasional churchgoers. Some of them

later told me that until Father Kiefer arrived, they had
an unexplainable feeling that they were missing out on
something—something big.

> *I'm not satisfied with this. What can I do to change
> this?*

In the five years Father Kiefer was at the parish, he estab-
lished a men's group and a women's group. They studied
orthodox books, brought in speakers, and attended Mass
and retreats together. He assisted the parish youth group,
the Cub Scouts, and the Boy Scouts. "The rule was: every
scout gets every Catholic medal available. When we run
out, we'll make stuff up," says Father Kiefer. He made
up a soldier medal and called it the "Put on the Armor
of Christ" medal. Father was also chaplain of the football
team at a local Catholic high school. Lastly, he rolled up
his cassock sleeves to revamp the languishing marriage
prep. Instead of a "life skills" class, where couples learned
to keep separate checkbooks, in addition to an "Agape
Service" (I do not want to know what this is), he offered
a holy hour, confessions, and a discussion of what the
sacrament of Matrimony really means.

But all these programs were not the essence of his
success. I saw him reach out to every person.

His reach extended beyond the parish boundaries when he invited me on one of the Women of Grace
retreats. It was some months after my seventh child was
born. Ideally, I wanted a more traditional retreat—something tough hosted by the likes of St. Ignatius. But I'll
admit that I gave that up the moment Father said, "You
probably need a weekend off." Probably? I'm there!

✳

I enter my cell. There is a soft lamp, a warm radiator, and an oversized, white bed. Obviously it's not designed for hermits, who like to invent penitential ways to lose sleep. Mothers do that year round without any help. Another welcome sight is the desk. Unlike my desk at home, the wood shows—there are no papers, hairbrushes, or socks covering it up. There is, however, a giant, homemade, frosted cookie shaped like a snowflake and wrapped up in cellophane, with a pretty note attached. I would like to buy a postcard of the desk, as a memento of my visit to this oasis of comfort and order.

There are more pretty notes piled neatly on my bed. Each is addressed to me from a different retreat leader, and each describes the six months of prayers and penances that she has done for me. Several ladies have given up chocolate, a few, caffeine. Together they've strung enough Rosaries to wrap around the retreat center.

Back downstairs there is a wine-and-cheese reception. A retreat leader named Lisa makes me feel welcome. Other ladies give talks under the direction of Father Kiefer. There is the Divine Office. There is Mass. There is Eucharistic adoration. There is confession. It is custom on retreat to give a general confession, reviewing not just recent sins but also old, encrusted ones. I go and finally renounce a long, deeply held sin—which, until that moment, I hadn't fully realized was a sin.

I am not the only one. Some of the retreat leaders talk about last year's retreat when they renounced their long, deeply held sins. They cry a lot, and there are tissue boxes all over the place. It makes me squirm. "So Father," I venture, after watching women dissolve for a day and a half. "You don't have tissue boxes decorating your men's retreats, do you?" I'm too cool for this party. He laughs.

At the end of the day, my tears catch up to theirs. I'm sure glad St. Ignatius isn't there to see it.

✳

Retreats such as the one I attended went on even after Father Joel was transferred to a new parish. He had made sure that others were trained to carry on the work. Popular as he was, this was never supposed to be about him— but about Christ.

This ideal of building something solid and enduring, while not counting his own personal glory, is something Father Joel talked about once in one of his military-themed sermons. He told the story of when he was at a field-training exercise with the order to secure the perimeter. This involves digging a foxhole. Cadet Kiefer dug his in a hurry. What did he care? He figured he wouldn't see it again anyway. Indeed, he did not. But the foxhole he inherited from another cadet named Chuck was large, airy, and clean. It was "the Taj Mahal of foxholes." Cadet Kiefer was ashamed, and he resolved that from then on he would only build well.

It's the kind of lesson that would have been lost on most people. But he could recognize it because he had eyes to see. It was the same sort of natural virtue he grew up seeing from his father, and it was the kind his father expected of him. He was instructed to say, "Yes, sir," and "No, sir," "Stand up straight," and "Open the door for your mother." Father's dad even had the kids practice answering the phone. "Hello, this is the Kiefer residence, Joel speaking." There was a sense of the rightness and wrongness of things, not limited to morality.

To me, John Kiefer sounds as if he could fill in for Napoleon on his day off—except that he was a praying man. Being naturally gifted with physical and mental strength can make a man forget the need for God. He can rely on his "own" powers. Joel saw his naturally gifted father submit himself to the Source of strength. Mass on Sundays was nonnegotiable. In spite of scouting trips, one full weekend a month, year round, there was never talk of "taking the day off from Mass." Mr. Kiefer simply herded the troop of woods-grimy boys into the back pews where their collective smell would cause the least offense. Back in the woods, he led the boys in prayer before eating. It didn't matter how hungry they were after a day of rock climbing, survival training, or latrine digging. They could wait a few moments and give thanks for their food. To this day, at the overflow Christmas Masses held in the church basement, Mr. Kiefer may be found kneeling on the hard floor—one of five or six men out of hundreds who don't.

And Mrs. Kiefer? I'm left wondering about her after all this man-centered talk. What was she like? There are two parts to the word "gentleman." If Mr. Kiefer made the man, it was Mrs. Kiefer who made the gentle.

Carol Kiefer's world was her home. Her horizons were the boundaries of her neighborhood. St. Bede's parish and school were just a five-minute walk away. She decorated the family culture in simple ways such as having the kids take piano lessons and by singing and playing games with them. She was, like my own mom, planted and rooted in the home, giving air, warmth, beauty, and life to all who lived there.

She appears to have been an avid holy-card collector, like me. Only, she actually used her stash. Mine is in a deep drawer—as if someday people are going to start paying cash for them. Look, a rare Hildegard of Bingen! Only ten grand! Mom Kiefer sent them to son Joel while he was away from home. The message was clear: be good. She also used the standard-issue "Devout Mother's Worn-Out Prayer Book" and looked often on a Sacred Heart statue, which oversaw the dirty dishes. I think the Mary statue that I have in my kitchen makes more sense. We all know from the Martha-and-Mary story that Jesus didn't do dishes.

Father Joel remembers sports on the school field and scouts in the auditorium. He grew up serving mass frequently. During summers, he worked in the rectory answering phones. He got to know all the priests and nuns well—with their human likes and dislikes. The possibility of joining their ranks was never *weird*. The setup seems to have nurtured several other vocations as well: there were several families in the neighborhood with members in religious life.

He himself began thinking about the priesthood in third grade when, he says, "I betrothed myself to Sister Matthew." She was the one. But it's not what you think. She was not the young, beautiful Sister of a boyhood crush. Father Joel explains:

> It was through her that the Holy Spirit showed me the Church as a bride and mother. Sister Matthew did not seem to have a husband like my mother. So I carried her books, opened doors for her, and walked her to the convent. I gave her presents. At scouts I made a wooden spoon with flowers, a Mother's Day craft. I brought it home and my mother thought it was for her. I had to tell her it was for Sister Matthew.

I wonder if Carol kept that moment and pondered it in her heart.

To a non-Catholic reader, this idea of the Church as bride and mother might sound bizarre. It will indeed take some explaining, like all the great mysteries of our Faith. Though I am not a theologian, here is my best attempt. People might believe that we Catholics take something real—like marriage—and dream up "something greater": such as the priesthood of Christ as bridegroom of the Church or the religious life of a sister representing the Church as mother and bride. C. S. Lewis put this concept into the witch's mouth in the Narnia book *The Silver Chair*: "*You have seen* lamps, and so *you* imagined a bigger and better lamp and called it the *sun*." Actually, it is just the opposite. The "something greater" is the reality and is reflected in the material. Christ is real—eternally real. Natural marriage is great, but it is for this world only. Even sacramental marriage ends with this world. Christ's marriage to the Church, and the priest's or nun's participation in that, is eternal.

When Father Joel entered the seminary, it was the best of times and the worst of times. It was right in the middle of the priest scandals of 1998. On the other hand, that series of events took away all the superfluous reasons for becoming a priest. There was no worldly glory in it. Father Kiefer recalls, "Everyone said, 'Why become a priest? Are you crazy? You're walking into a mess.'" Joel's father asked him a round of pointed questions. Then both parents gave him their blessing. They had given him a sense of honor and seen it tested in combat missions in Somalia and Haiti. The sacrifice then was for a temporal homeland. This time it was for an eternal one.

"Especially now in the priesthood today there has to be a holy boldness." I saw him call this boldness out from the young men of a congregation once. He challenged them to be part of something "manly, holy, and danger-ous." Not the military, the priesthood.

Father says he looks forward to getting old so he can finally say whatever he wants and chalk it up to senility. But I believe that even when the close-cropped hair is gray or gone, he will always retain a youthful boldness, even as his father continues to kneel on the hard floor.

Saying Yes to Strength

The Church is feminine—she is *mater* (mother), the one who brings forth Christ, and mysteriously is also bride, the one who receives Christ. Yet, the Church often expresses her faith in a characteristically manly way. In her infancy, she was baptized in blood. Several of her early popes were martyrs. Down through the ages, she shows a moral force backed up by action and bravery.

Guys respect this stuff. You know what? So do I. I'm a typical woman. I enjoy fashion, dancing, and gabbing with my girlfriends. Yet, my favorite saints are Jesuit–martyr types. They are like James Bond—only, they are spying for God. Outwitting their enemies. Brave. Daring. Adventurous.

I was lucky that my older brother Ben told me the lives of the saints and martyrs at bedtime while I was growing up. Otherwise, I would not have heard about them. It was the era of softness and niceness. We were often told that the Church needed a woman's touch. Unfortunately, it came out more like a preschooler's—green-felt banners, clowns, and the sort of music we sang while holding hands in a circle in kindergarten:

Here we are, all together, as we sing our song, joyfully.

With *"Here we are,"* a lot of guys said, "There I go!" Churchgoing was not for men. It became something that women and children did.

Years passed. The lack of men in church took its toll. In 1994, the ever-efficient Swiss published a survey with these startling findings. If Mom goes to church and Dad does not, only 2 percent of the children grow up to be regular churchgoers. If Dad goes to church and Mom does not, then between 66 and 75 percent of the children will end up as churchgoers.* The conclusion, then, is that when Mom alone takes the kids to church, they tend to see it as kid stuff—just like when she takes them to birthday parties with green-felt banner crafts, clowns, and kindergarten songs. When Dad goes, they see it as a grown-up activity.

All his life, Father Joel saw his strong dad submit himself to the Faith. His dad never skipped Sunday Mass because he had something better to do. To this day, the man won't even sit down—as his age permits—when he prays at Mass. He kneels on the hard floor just as he always has. He not only taught his son to keep the Faith, he trained him to serve in a way the Jesuit martyr types did—with strength, courage, and a sense of adventure. This is the kind of priest that attracts men back to church, and women, too.

Tell your children the lives of the saints. Show them the bravery of the saints, how they risked everything,

---

* Robbie Low, "The Truth about Men and Church," *Touchstone Magazine*, June 2003, http://www.touchstonemag.com/archives/article.php?id=16-05-024-v.

put up with anything, and counted their own comfort as nothing. Practice the fasts prescribed by the Church. Perform the works of mercy with the kids so that they will have some experience sacrificing for a greater purpose. Give them a faith they can take seriously—worth living and dying for.

For Better,
for Worse

Saying Yes to Spiritual Poverty

Sister Marie José de la Rosa, S.C.C.

Not my way, but God's.

You never run into nuns these days. The exception is if you are in Rome and they are coming at you full throttle because you are between them and the Holy Father. Then it's more like they are running into you.

In that case, an interview is out of the question.

If you do want to connect with them—in a purely electronic, non–body slam sort of way—you have to contact the convent. That is fine, except if all the nuns you know prefer to communicate via the telephone booth down at the grocer's (which went out of business thirty-five years ago) and then only in emergencies.

It was four months left to deadline, and I was coming up short on sisters for this book. That was how I ended up settling for Sister Marie José de la Rosa of the Sisters of Christian Charity—not to imply there is anything wrong with her. She is fabulous: twenty-two years young, highly intelligent, radiating peace and joy even over the phone. Best of all, she possesses her own e-mail account. It's just that I had never met her, and this was against my policy for this book.

My friend Dan, a local reporter, had interviewed her just before she left for the convent at age seventeen. It was he who tossed her into my lap. Luckily she had spent the past five years fasting, or it might have hurt.

Thank God he did. Sister brings something completely new to this project. Her home life stands in stark contrast to that of the cohesive, unified Rocks. But there is a hidden strength in her family that I think the Rocks would envy.

How many Catholic families do you know who struggle? I mean really struggle with all the things that terrorize us in the night—poverty, apostasy, disability, and not least, divorce? That was Sister Marie José de la Rosa's family. In fact, it still is. Sister's parents, Joe (José) and Adnery, do not glow in the dark like those hollow plastic Mary statues sold in gift-shop value bins. Their goodness is solid even though they struggle to this day.

Adnery de la Rosa is a pious, devout, Puerto Rican matriarch, but she never had time to pray the way her heart desired. While the family was still quite young, Joe became permanently disabled. He was working on a cabinet at his job as a maintenance worker when a fall against the corner shattered one side of his face. Even with reconstructive surgery, he never fully recovered. He became depressed. It fell to Mrs. de la Rosa to provide.

Sister—whose baptismal same was Sara—is too respectful of her father to say much about it. "He was very quiet, very internal, and grew more so after the accident." She believes it hurt him deeply that he could no longer provide.

Mrs. de la Rosa had always worked outside the home. It wasn't an option of convenience but of necessity. Money had always been tight. After the accident, it was pulled even tighter. With three kids to care for—Sara and her two brothers, José and David—Mrs. de la Rosa had to get a second job. Even so, the family ate potatoes—often—and made decisions about whether to go out based on whether they could pay for the gas.

Mrs. de la Rosa was simply not home enough hours in the day to corral the family together for a nightly Rosary. But she was a woman of deep prayer. She had a personal habit of getting up early to read the scriptures. As often as she could, she talked to the children about the urgency of prayer. "We have to pray. God's not in our schools; God's not in the world. How can people live without God?"

Mr. de la Rosa, though disabled, did what he could. He took on some of the home duties and many of the out-of-home duties, such as driving the kids to activities. He never complained. Since buying toys was out of the question, he invented them. All the kids were into softball, so he drilled a hole in a ball and hung it from the porch roof. Voila—batting practice. "We look back. He was so resourceful," Sister says.

Yet, each period of financial desperation was a terrible strain on the marriage. As my Irish mother-in-law used to say, "When poverty comes in the front door, love goes out the back."

It is unfortunately very common for a disability to ruin a marriage. People may vow to stick together "in sickness and in health," but most of us think in terms of a twenty-four-hour flu. Many couples crack under the strain of a long-term disability. The sick person gets depressed. The caregiver becomes overwhelmed. Sister speaks of a moment in her teens when things were so bad that her mom took her aside and told her she was seriously considering her options. There was only one thing holding her back—her children. Young Sara was shocked. Yet, her mom was not threatening. She was not even complaining. Actually, she was making Sara a promise. She was saying, "Not my way, but God's."

Years ago, a friend on the brink of divorce said the opposite to me: "It's every man for himself." Not Mom de la Rosa. Her ship might have been sinking, but she refused to abandon it. She was not getting on that lifeboat without everybody, heavy and weighed down as it might be. She had been defending the kids all their lives. Her son José nearly died at birth. He's a twin, and they had come too early. José was only one pound. His sister did not survive. Then there was David—in every way a normal boy. Then at age eleven he went blind. Sister calls it a "fluke," meaning no one could figure it out. His suffering caused him to ask the eternal question, "Why, God?" He pulled away from the Faith. To Mom de la Rosa, the kids had been through enough pain. She would not take the cross off her own shoulders and lay it on theirs.

Sara's dad did his best to keep the marriage together, too. "He took it day by day." Joe was not a devout man. He was raised as a Jehovah's Witness and became a Catholic, but after a couple of years, he stopped going to Mass. I ask Sister why, since this is not standard convert behavior. Usually they want to go out and baptize people on street corners. For a moment, Sister and I speculate. She offers that perhaps the short session of Rite of Christian Initiation of Adults (RCIA) just wasn't enough. I, who recently attended what looked like a mariachi Mass, suggest that perhaps the effusive expression of faith in the Puerto Rican community just didn't appeal to his quiet temperament. "Maybe," she says, and we move on. It doesn't seem to be the thing at their house to dissect people's consciences at the kitchen table. She is certain of one thing, though. "There was a Christlike spirit of sacrifice for the family in all he did."

Because of their poverty, Mr. and Mrs. de la Rosa wanted all their kids to go to college and have an opportunity at careers. Sara loved medicine. It was her parents' dream that she become a doctor. She was accepted to the highly selective University of Notre Dame. She was to be the first college graduate in the family and very possibly the one who would lift them out of poverty.

How was she going to tell them about her vocation? She'd had an attraction to the Sisters of Christian Charity for years. They taught her in first grade. "I loved them. I looked at other communities, but it was hard. I knew it was right with them. I felt at home," Sister recalls.

This makes sense when you consider the fact that this religious community's focus is very much like the home Sara came from. Since 1849, their mission has been to show Christlike love to the world. The foundress, Mother

Pauline, cared for the blind and the poor of Germany. The sisters teach school and tend the sick. Similarly, at home Sara was the big sister. With Mom out of the house much of the time, she was teacher and nurse to the boys. They went to her with their problems. She helped them with their homework. She fixed things that were broken and patched them up when they got hurt.

Mrs. de la Rosa, too, saw her daughter's vocation as bearing a close resemblance to the home—perhaps a bit too close. When Sara finally did tell her mom, she was not happy. Poverty nearly destroyed them and now Sara wanted to take a vow of it? "Mom wasn't exposed to sisters. She didn't have a good understanding of what they were. She thought the vow of poverty meant destitution, the evil of poverty," she explains. "Please, God," Sara's mother prayed, "I already gave you one daughter." Yet, neither parent tried to stop her from entering. "Not my way, but God's."

Actually, Sara's mom had helped prepare her for this particular community, whose charism is transformation through the Blessed Sacrament. "I can always remember how my mom acted in chapel," Sister says. "I can always see her deep in prayer before the Blessed Sacrament."

I ask her if growing up so poor gave her a head start in convent life. "There are two types of poverty," she tells me. "The material I find it pretty easy to be without—not to have my own car, not to have what I like to eat. Now I'm learning that it's about spiritual poverty as well."

I ask her what her family thinks of her vocation, now that five years have passed. She laughs. The "boys," who are now young men, pout a bit when she can come home only for a weekend at a time. Both parents continue to ask, "Are you happy? Are you happy?" "Yes," she answers, "I am happy." They just want to be sure.

Sister's dad, still not a practicing Catholic, finds a way to express faith through her. "God has a special plan for you. The grace of God is at work in you."

And what about the marriage, the one constant after all the years of struggle? The de la Rosas are still together. That's the first thing. When something holy is threatened with destruction, you want to cheer about its survival. When you find out that it is well again, you want to weep. With the kids grown and taking care of themselves, Sister says her folks are able to "concentrate on their relationship."

Does she mean candlelight dinners, vacations, hand holding on the beach?

"Uh, no," she laughs. "There's still no money for that, and Mom still works two jobs. It's just that now there is a sense that they've made it. They've survived the worst of it. They sit down together, talk, laugh, share, and even tease each other. They've entered a new phase of their lives."

Saying Yes to Spiritual Poverty

We once owned this DVD player that worked only part of the time. It used to freeze up randomly. You then had to stop everything, pop the disc out, shut the DVD player off, turn it back on, pop the thing back in, and then find your way back to where you were supposed to be. You never knew when this was going to happen. Everything could be fine and then right while the hero was in mid-leap from a burning building, the picture would freeze. I couldn't wait for it to break completely so we could justify getting a new one. I showed it to my dad, an engineer, and he said that the problem was that the manufacturer had put it into production before it was ready. If you got a later version of the same DVD player, you were fine. It wouldn't do that freezing up thing because somebody had noticed it and fixed it.

I think that goes for a lot of marriages.

I got the later version of my parents' marriage. I'm the eighth and last child, so by the time I came along, it would seem that they had worked through all the production glitches.

There was no freezing up, popping out, shutting off, and finding your way back to where you were supposed to be. Breaking was out of the question. Starting over with a new one? Impossible. Mom and Pop were just two peaceful, slightly boring people who liked each other, liked working together (whether in our massive garden or teaching catechism), and who were so united they seemed like two halves of the same person. My mom's half did the talking; my dad's half looked for his glasses.

Oh, and their date night was a novena.

I am grateful that I grew up this way. Yet I must also confess that for years it drove me absolutely crazy that Greg and I didn't have my parents' marriage. I figured theirs just rolled off the assembly line perfect. I didn't realize that maybe it was so good because they'd patiently worked through the production glitches long before I came along. You know how some people are raised with wealth so they expect to have their parents' income right away, forgetting that their parents started marriage in a basement apartment with two borrowed chairs? I was like that, only I was used to a wealth of virtue. I wanted it handed to me, not to have to sacrifice for years to get it. The world tells us that it's normal for marriages to break and be replaced. We live in a disposable society. When the DVD player malfunctions, you throw it away.

Consider the de la Rosas' marriage—at its worst point, many people would have said to junk it. The de la Rosas chose to work out all the glitches instead—the poverty, the illness, the unending work, and perhaps the feeling of personal loneliness when they couldn't turn to each other for comfort—a word which literally means "to give strength to." Their strength lay in these words: "Not my way, but God's."

That is the spiritual poverty Sister says she is now learning to live in the convent. I would never have guessed with her background that this is what she struggles with the most. "I pray for it every single day," she says.

Spiritual poverty is one of those gifts that you have to pray for because there is no other way you will want it. Sister describes it as keeping your hands open:

> That's what my novice directress would say. We have to keep them open for God to take whatever it is he wants, not because he is mean, but because it could be standing between you and him if you grasp it too tightly. As I prayed and prayed about it, I came to realize that by opening your hands, you could be possibly opening them up to nails, just as Christ's hands were open to nails. It hurts, but it is how we are united to Christ.

I find this terrifying. If you've ever been through extreme pain, the last thing it feels like is beautiful. I am reminded of a scene in the movie *Entertaining Angels* about Dorothy Day. Dorothy witnesses a friend, a young woman she has fought hard to save, die on the street. All her efforts lost, she gives in to exhaustion and anger. She runs into a nearby church, confronts a large bloody crucifix, and screams, "You're ugly! How could anyone love you?" Yet, she goes out to the poor once again, to love him in his wretchedness. That is spiritual poverty.

That is the vocation God chose for Sister Marie José. That is what he prepared for her. That was what Mom and Dad de la Rosa cooperated with—whether they knew it or not.

I think of all those times Mrs. de la Rosa longed to pray, intended to pray, or regretted not being able to pray. You know what? She *was* praying. Prayer is the lifting of the mind and heart to God. St. Francis de Sales explains it this way:

> You tell me that you do not have the time to give two or three hours to prayer; who asks you to do so? Recommend yourself to God the first thing in the morning . . . and then go about your affairs, resolved nevertheless to raise your spirit to God even amidst company. Who can prevent you from speaking to him in the depths of your heart? (*The Heart of Prayer*)

You know what else? I think that each time Sister's dad tells her that God has a plan for her, he is renewing his acceptance of God's will. And he does so, not just for her, but also for himself. He is opening his hands and saying, "Take all my hopes; take my beloved daughter." As he says to Sara, "The grace of God is at work in you," so also can she say, "And in you, Dad."

The grace of the sacrament of Matrimony is not just a poetic phrase. It is real—more real than our problems, our glitches. If they seem frustrating and unfixable, that's because we can't fix them ourselves. Mrs. de la Rosa teaches me that it takes a divine engineer to fix them. We just have to hand it off to him and say, Not my way, but God's.

The Divine
Liturgy

Saying Yes to Inheritance

Father Mark Fesniak,
Ukrainian Archdiocese of Philadelphia

**There has to be something
better than this.**

One Sunday morning when he was about eighteen, my husband, Greg, drove through the "City of Man" into the rough section of town and walked up a flight of steep, stone steps. He entered the doors of a dingy city duplex that had been converted into a Ukrainian Catholic Church and found himself in the "City of God." The Divine Liturgy was in progress—that's the Eastern Rite term for what we call "Mass" in the Western or Latin Rite Catholic Church. The Ukrainian is one of the Eastern or Byzantine Rites within the Catholic Church. If you've ever seen an Eastern liturgy, you know it is very beautiful, very mystical, very ornate, and all around very "very." If you haven't seen one, well, get going.

The Eastern liturgy is nearly identical with that of the Russian Orthodox Church and the other national "Orthodox" churches of Eastern Europe. The difference is that Eastern Catholics are united under the authority of Rome. They are fully Catholic.

Greg was so taken with the Divine Liturgy that he decided to join the Ukrainian Catholic Church. He has never looked back.

The only thing wrong with Eastern Rite churches, as far as I can see, is the same thing wrong nearly everywhere in the Church: there is a priest shortage. The Ukrainian Rite is the second-largest rite in the Catholic Church, and it routinely allows married men to become priests. So, to people who think celibacy is why we have a priest shortage, think again. In the Ukrainian church that Greg and I attend, often it seems that our priests are barely unpacked before they're shuffled off again. Our parish is used to this frequent changing of the guard. We simply buy two cakes. One is presented as a farewell to the outgoing pastor—with a grateful, affectionate round of "*Mnohaya Lita*" ("God grant him many years!"). The other cake is for the following Sunday—to welcome the new pastor. Strike up another round of "*Mnohaya Lita*"!

It was different with Father Mark. When news of his impending transfer came, our normally docile group of bishop-abiding citizens raised a protest. Somebody handed me a petition. It went something like this: "Dear Your Excellency, you promised us that Father Mark would stay for at least two years. You owe us at least another six months." I signed.

The protest was short-lived. Much embarrassed, Father Mark stepped in and gently confiscated the document. "When your bishop says go," he said, "you drop everything and go. It's the voice of God."

The voice of God—he knew it well. He had heard it before, on an early morning commute to his job as East Coast manager for the fashion empire Jones New York. He had what almost anyone would consider a great life in the "City of Man." But as he sat in his car, waiting to go through the Lincoln Tunnel, the thought suddenly came to him, "There's got to be something better than this."

He went to work and asked for a year's leave of absence. Where did he want to go that could be better than New York? Los Angeles? London? Paris?

Home. To Mom and Dad, and the foundations of his faith in the coal-mine region of Pennsylvania. Growing up in a family of four children, Mark Fesniak had often thought about becoming a priest. He and his twin brother, Joe, served at the altar—a lot. "The doubles," as their mom called them, did double the service most altar boys did. Mom, Mary Fesniak, was Eastern Rite and Dad, Henry, was Western Rite. So on any given Sunday, the boys served the 8 a.m. Mass at their dad's church and then the 10 a.m. Divine Liturgy at their mom's church. It felt perfectly natural to practice both rites. (The Lloyd kids know the feeling.)

Father Mark says that both pastors were a big influence on him because of their long years in the parishes. He fondly remembers the Ukrainian pastor, Father Radchuk, taking him with a group of children up to the choir loft and having them sail paper airplanes down into the church. This definitely gets a raised eyebrow from me. I'm used to churches where you enter quietly, tiptoe to your seat, genuflect, and slide to your knees. The worst you get is a row of old men and ladies who chitchat in church—a practice which seems to run through that population like arthritis. But at least they stage whisper: "*Missed you at BINGO Thursday night.*"

The atmosphere in Eastern Rite churches is completely different. There are often several conversations going on at once before the Divine Liturgy and after. It's not laxity. It's more like warm familiarity. Even so, the parishioners at young Mark's church thought flying airplanes in church a bit much. To them, Father Radchuk replied, "The children are playing at Jesus' house today." The experience was meant to make the kids feel affection, rather than fear, for our Lord. To this day, Father Mark cherishes the memory.

Mark played with Jesus at home, too. "My mother found Joe trying to nail me to a tree. He had a hammer and nails," he recalls. Perhaps there was some foreshadowing in the moment. She would someday offer her son up as another Christ, through the priesthood. The roots of her maternal offering were intertwined with her strong devotion to Our Lady.

Mom practiced all the Marian feasts with gusto. On Our Lady's greatest feast, the Dormition (also known as the Assumption), it is the custom to bless flowers. Mark's mom dried the blessed flowers and used them throughout the year as sacramentals—material aids in prayer and devotion. (Right—so much for thinking I'm pious by letting them compost in a corner of the yard instead of putting them in the garbage.) She would throw them into the coal stove and burn them on fearsome, stormy nights. When young Mark suffered one of his asthma attacks, she would place them under his pillow and pray the *Bohoroditsya*, the Hail Mary.

Her prayers were not for times of need only. She prayed as she worked throughout her day, by singing. "My mom sang around the house all the time, hymns to the Mother of God in Slavonic and Ukrainian," says Father Mark.

Mark's dad also had a steadfast devotion to Our Lady. His favorite devotion to her was the Latin Rite prayer, the Rosary. It was often wrapped around his hand as he went about his day. "I'm praying it for you guys," he would tell his children.

It was Mark's dad who trained Mark and his siblings to behave well at Mass when they were very small. (Ah, the tiptoe, genuflect, and slide to your knees choreography.) Father Mark said Dad had another motive for taking the kids to church. "He wanted Mom to stay home and get dinner ready."

After putting in a solid morning in company with the Lord at two liturgies, the rest of Sunday was a family affair. The Fesniaks always ate a big meal together.

Their sense of ritual carried over into weekdays as well. "In our town the big Ukrainian dome had a cross on top with a light on it. Mom watched nightly for the light, and when it came on, it was bedtime," recalls Father Mark. Imagine your earliest recollections as a small child, going to bed when God decides.

There was only one problem with it. God delegated "Operation Light Switch" to a man named John. Sometimes John forgot all about it. As the twins shook the house foundations in the riot that always preceded bedtime, Mark's mom impatiently dialed the phone. "For heaven's sake, John, turn on that light!"

Faith, for Mark, was like this. It permeated every day. It permeated the whole year. This is something so ingrained in Eastern Rite Catholics that they even greet one another according to the liturgical season.

An everyday greeting sounds phonetically like this:

> *SLA-va Ee-SOO-soo Khris-TOO.* (Glory be to Jesus Christ.)
>
> Response: *SLA-va ee na VEE-ki.* (Glory forever.)

At Christmas:

> *Khris-TOS razh-DAyetsya!* (Christ is born!)
>
> Response: *SlaVEEti Yoho!* (Glorify him!) (Or, if you've done your Advent fasting: Pass the *Yohos!*)

At Easter:

> *Khris-TOS voss-KRESS.* (Christ is risen!)
>
> Response: *Vo EE-stin-nu voss-KRESS!* (Truly he is risen!)

Easter is the time of greatest rejoicing for Ukrainians. Christ has conquered death! He is risen! We have survived another Lent!

Father Mark's mom was into Lent like nobody's business. Since Jesus led the way with forty days of megapenance in the desert—including, but not limited to, starvation—Mary Fesniak thought that the least her family could do was attend every single Lenten service in both rites. These services are mainly the Stations of the Cross in the West and the *Akafist* (a hymn service involving a penitential amount of standing) in the East. Mom had a parallel policy regarding fasts. In the Eastern Rites, discipline has been modified somewhat in recent years. But for strict fast days, the no-dairy rule persists. If you ask me, the official greeting on those days should be: "Peanut butter AGAIN-ski!" Still, what the laity endure is peanuts to what is required of the priest, including fasting and lengthy, multiple liturgies (many priests serve more than one parish). By the end of Christmas or Easter, the priest is ready to do a "Rip van Winkle-ski" and take a twenty-year nap. Could this be the reason that Father Mark admits to suppressing his childhood attraction to the priesthood? No wonder.

Yet, it's no wonder it came back to him while waiting in a long line of cars approaching the Lincoln Tunnel. It is in the silent moments of waiting, when time stands still, when activity ceases, that God speaks: "There's got to be something better than this." Mark knew there was because he had seen it, the better world. He had lived within its walls as a child. How keen the contrast between the two worlds: the world of success—with its demands on body and soul, its dividends in material goods, which thieves may break in and steal and moth and rust corrode—and the world he came from, with the steady rhythm of the liturgical year, with its demands of body and soul, its dividends immaterial and everlasting.

Father Mark tells me that when he returned home in his thirties, he wasn't thinking specifically of priesthood yet, just retreat and discernment. His mom wondered what it was all about and exclaimed, "You're never gonna let us die in peace!" But she was pleased when he started making himself useful at her parish. In a small parish this consists of everything from teaching catechism to making hundreds of pierogies to keep the parish solvent. It was during this time that the pastor told him he would make a good priest. It was the voice of God.

In 2003, at the age of forty, Mark Fesniak was ordained and shortly afterward given leadership of our parish. In 2005, he baptized our sixth girl, Melanie. It wasn't long afterward that we got word that Father Mark was moving on.

The archbishop heard about our failed petition, and just before Father Mark's departure, our parish got a special letter. It said that he understood why we would want to hang on to Father Mark, and there were no hard feelings. But the facts of the case were that Father Mark was needed. He was young. There were three parishes plus a school to manage. Not only that, but the archbishop was sending him back to the coal regions to be near his family. His twin brother, Joe, was battling liver disease, and his mother had pancreatic cancer.

By the end of the letter, all plans to renew the petition were off. The archbishop had reminded us that Father Mark was just a loan. He belonged to others. He must go where the Church needed him. As a Catholic, I understood that. Then there was his family. They needed him, too. As a mother, I understood that as well.

In 2007, he stood by his father and siblings during his mother's final illness. She lived long enough to enjoy the traditional "holy supper" on Christmas Eve. This is a family ritual rich in symbolism. Ukrainians lay straw over their best tablecloth, and in the center are placed three loaves of braided bread and a lighted candle. They eat a twelve-course supper in honor of the twelve apostles.

All the dishes are meatless, non-dairy foods in remembrance of the Christ Child who was born in poverty and deprivation to save the world. (In recent decades, it also commemorates the starvation of the Ukrainian people by the millions under Soviet dictator Josef Stalin in the 1930s.) During the supper, the family feels united to its living and dead members.

Father Mark's mom ate the holy supper with the help of an elderly sister who once taught her when she was a child. Then the family got her to the Christmas Eve services she so loved. She sang "God Eternal," a hymn as familiar to Ukrainians as "Silent Night" is to us:

> *God Eternal, to us is born*
> *He came down, from above*
> *To reveal His perfect love*
> *And to save the world*

She sang all the verses, verses that Father Mark never knew existed, that she knew from the old country. Father Mark remembers thinking, "Next year at this time, she'll be singing in heaven."

A few days later, surrounded by her family with a statue of the Blessed Virgin at her bedside, she was anointed by her son. She could die in peace. She had shown Father Mark the sureness, the goodness, the realness of life as a citizen of the City of God, and now with his help, she was going to meet the Mother she had sung to all those years.

Saying Yes to Inheritance

Not long ago I took my little girl and boy to a party where I didn't know anyone outside of the host family. Meeting a whole pile of strangers all in one shot is not my

favorite thing, unless they happen to be my own kind—
either Catholics or homeschoolers, or at least drivers of
beat-up Suburbans. Nope. All we had uniting us was a
Saturday afternoon of sedentary babysitting. I don't know
about you, but Saturday is the day I deal with all the
work that backs up from Sunday through Friday. I took
a look around at the well-dressed guests. Perhaps they
too longed for home and the comforts of hauling dead
leaves and twigs to the curb. Maybe I could get a support
group going, I thought. Nope again. Deep sharing is not
the order of the day at these events. Chitchat is.

The chitchat went at a steady clip until someone nod-
ded approvingly at me and said, "She has two children,"
indicating the mere two I had brought with me: the requi-
site boy and girl, dressed in party clothes, playing nicely,
betraying nothing of beat-up Suburbans. I knew that if I
confessed to having five more kids besides, it would mess
up my glistening reputation. So, of course, I did it.

Their first reaction was wonderment that I was not
built like a tractor. Then came admiration that, with some
grown children, I look a sight younger than the prophet-
ess Anna. "Just one husband?" someone ventured. Yes,
only one sire was employed in this vast familial under-
taking. Admiration turned to amazement. Finally, it came
out that our son was born last. "That's it!" a man shouted,
as if he'd cracked the code, solved the mystery, and won
the game. The numerous girls must therefore have been
mere attempts at "spiritual completeness" in son-having.
Of course.

After that, nobody but the kindly old uncle would
talk to me. Interest in my intimate life cooled to about
the temperature of an ice pick. I tried to keep the chitchat
flowing by asking about them and their interests. This is

a widely accepted way of getting people to prop up their end of a conversation or simply take over one. But they merely smiled and said as few words as possible. They were not taking any chances that I might be contagious.

I'm used to this sort of thing. I've even considered handing out scripts to save people trouble, such as the following:

> Me: I have seven kids. I may look like a normal person, but I am really a mindless, maniacal, breeding machine, an alien from a planet that destroyed its ecosystem with diapers. Yours is next.
>
> Them: No! (Gasp. Stagger. Eye pop.)

It doesn't usually get me down, but this time it did. You see, these people were Catholics, or had at least started out that way. They were the children and grandchildren of hard-working immigrants. Uncle was telling me all about the parish in his old neighborhood. It sounded like a blast—kids, families, noise, laughter, with a Bells of St. Mary's school staffed by young, lively nuns. That was years ago. The family had long moved away from that neighborhood. Now they were "better off" with nicer houses, voluntary sterility, and cold, dismissive smiles, denoting membership in country clubs that would have thrown their grandparents out. Are we having fun yet?

Later, as I led my children home, my hand went involuntarily to my heart. I wanted to clutch my faith, holding its preciousness tight within me. Familiar images flashed through my imagination: my grandmother, a quiet, serious, dutiful soul, walking to Mass every day, even in her eighties on a bad hip; the two-hour Ukrainian funeral of Greg's grandmother, who kept her word and raised his mom Catholic, even though she was an unchurched Presbyterian, receiving the Faith through the hand of a Ukrainian priest a month before her death; my mom, lying on a rented hospital bed in our living room, choked with cancer to the point she could no longer talk, lifting herself up when the priest brought in the Blessed Sacrament and singing in Latin. This is my wealth, my heritage and my children's.

I got home and gathered the kids. Suddenly it felt urgent to tell them, "Don't let the Faith end with me. Don't let it end with you. Guard your inheritance and pass it down." A thing is considered precious for various reasons. Maybe it's rare, or costly, or exquisitely fashioned, or ancient, or belonged to someone we love. Our Faith is all those things.

Father Mark had an advantage over most Catholic Americans. He was raised, not only with the doctrines of Faith, but also with a culture of Faith. After the Baptism of St. King Vladimir in the year 988, Ukrainians spent the next millennium developing the Catholic communal life in all its fullness. In the home, in the parish, and in the nation, everyone, from peasant farmer to nobleman, sang the same songs, ate the same food, wore the same ceremonial dress, and marked time by the same liturgical year. They mourned when heaven mourned and rejoiced when heaven rejoiced.

This was also true of the other nations in Europe. But many, particularly those in the European Union, have since lost, squandered, or abandoned their Christian roots. Ukraine was too busy trying to survive. Her millennial roots were deep enough to sustain her people, even under the violent storms of Stalinism. Her roots were hardy enough to transplant in foreign soil, in the United States, and bring up new shoots.

This sense of continuity and belonging is still seen in the liturgy. All Christians gather family and friends to share in the celebration of a Baptism, but Ukrainians invite the saints to join in, too. The priest raises the child up to the icons of the saints along the walls, as if introducing him to his family beyond this world.

Culture is the expression of how a community lives and what it loves. It is everything that reminds people of why they're here on this earth. That is why Stalin attempted to smash it. Violence seemed efficient. It's quick, and you can always use the labor of the faithful to build their own prisons. Yet, violence was not enough. Here in the West, our way is more effective: to corrode Christian culture with a me-seeking materialism. People willingly labor to build prisons of their own making. A bewildered sense of unfulfillment is their only clue that something is wrong.

"There's got to be more than this." Yes. The generations of mothers and fathers, grandparents, and paperairplane priests showed Father Mark what that "something more" was. Even an act as simple as watching his father walk around the house with a Rosary wrapped around his hand signified a daily pilgrimage to heaven.

In 2011, when Henry Fesniak lay on his death bed, Father Mark put his Rosary around his Father's hands. He says, "He always had them in his hands. It did not seem right seeing him there without any. His heavenly Mother met him with those beads. I cherish them."

The sacramentality of the world surrounds us. Accept no substitutions. It is vital to experience God daily whether you come from a hostile Communist state, which seeks to steal and murder your inheritance, or from a no less hostile pleasure state, which seeks to seduce you with quick, cheap substitutes for real joy. Step into the City of God and claim your inheritance. Hold it tightly to your heart. Sing it, wear it, eat it, greet it. And if you happen to have access to a light on a church dome, tuck your kids into bed by it.

In the World,
Not of It

Saying Yes to the Greatest Commandment

Sister Mariana McGlynn, O.P.

You know where you are at home.

Sing it with me, Dionne—"What the world needs now are nuns, sweet nuns."

I am not going to stop singing this tune until I get the Dominican Sisters of Mary, Mother of the Eucharist, based in Ann Arbor, Michigan, to open one of their schools next door to me. You know who they are, right? Maybe you get their mail—the envelope that barely has room for your address because it's crowded with young sisters looking out at you, smiling competently. Printed on the outside is: "One convent with a different sort of 'vocations crisis.'"

Maybe you saw them on Oprah, talking about mystical stuff such as being married to Jesus, radiating peace and fulfillment, dispelling all prejudices about religious life being oppressive. Oprah said she wished she could be in their shoes, literally, as she waggled a steep stiletto at the camera. Their simplicity and authenticity seemed to grab her heart as well as her feet. She keeps in touch with them still.

I'm right there with her.

I am a homeschooler and—don't get me wrong—I am grateful for it. Now that I have three graduates, I can say with confidence that, in spite of me, it has been a success. I will refrain from bragging about my girls' successes in school and in the world (this isn't a Christmas letter). What matters more is that they are all committed Catholics. The proof is that they gripe faithfully whenever a fast day rolls around.

But I cannot deceive myself that our children have had the kind of formation at home that they could have had from a religious order such as these Dominicans. First, there is the scope of knowledge owned by a body of sisters, all specialists in their fields. Then there's the discipline. (Have any sisters ever announced the close of a school year as I once did, by tearing up the math worksheets and stomping on them?) But it's really just the whole setting. With six girls, our homeschool did once qualify as a mini convent. But imagine how it would it be if they'd been surrounded by dozens of young religious women, examples of total commitment to Christ!

I'll tell you how it would be (cue Dionne): "It would be as it was *meant* to be . . . as it once was . . . dedicated Sisters, hand in hand with families . . . building up the Church, transforming the world to the service of God and the betterment of the human race . . . my getting the ironing done." Are you feeling it? Sing it with me! "What the world needs now are nuns."

Pardon me for getting carried away. These attacks of holy envy come over me sometimes.

I'm completely jealous of the families that flow in and out of these nuns' schools every day in Michigan and other states. The parents arrive early in the morning to attend Mass with their children and the sisters. They stop by on First Fridays for Eucharistic adoration with younger babies in tow. Everybody wants to stay awhile. Even Oprah wants a piece of it—or is it a peace of it? Kick off the spike heels, and take a place reserved for you in this family, this community, this culture, this civilization.

Sister Mariana McGlynn is one of these sisters. Formerly known as Mary McGlynn (she's Polish, obviously), she is one of five children of Ann and Kevin McGlynn. A photo of the whole family, including Grandma Mary Jane Hathaway, taken on the day of Sister's first vows, shows that they all share the same full, open smile, as if they are right in the middle of a laugh.

They seem to share the ten talents, too. Sister Mariana's older sister Kathleen is a pro-life ob-gyn. This means she's got both the brains to become a doctor and the guts to tell her colleagues and patients that she won't prescribe contraception or do sterilizations. Younger sister Emily teaches down in Chile. Sister says she is the one who can go anywhere and get along with anybody, making converts in the process. Brothers James and John sound like modern-day Sons of Thunder. James is a naval flight officer, and John is following his footsteps at the Naval Academy.

Ann and Kevin sent their kids to Catholic school, then to public school. The kids were looked up to as leaders in sports, especially volleyball, basketball, and track. But Ann and Kevin knew well that they were surrounded by a culture that was hostile to the Faith—not just indifferent to it, but openly in conflict with it. "They wouldn't allow the culture to take over our priorities," says Sister. "We were used to standing out, not being afraid to go against what everyone was thinking." Mary's mom and dad were strict. The kids could only go to G or PG movies, they couldn't dress like everybody else, and they did not do sports on Sundays.

"Wait," you may be thinking. "I get the movies and clothes thing. But how is sports on Sunday a problem? Isn't that partly what Sunday is for, a little recreation?" Sports have a way of taking over your life, even when you are at peewee level. (I have a neighbor who is gone three afternoons a week just for one sport, and he's five.) What if you are the type of kid who stands to win a college scholarship, which was the case for all of the McGlynn kids, who were tall, strong, and fast? To them sports were more than recreation—they were career builders. What did they do, and what about the team? You've got to show up, right? "It became a problem in high school," Sister Mariana admits.

She played on a traveling volleyball team in tournaments out of town on a lot of weekends. She took some consolation in the fact that, even though she was the only

Catholic on the team, the coach respected her need to attend Mass on Sunday. Somebody always made sure to drive her, whether it was the coach or one of the parents. "It meant that other people were coming to a Catholic Mass who otherwise might never do that," she says. She kept up her commitment to the team and led other people to God. Sounds great!

But sports were destroying Sunday. Besides attending Mass, the McGlynns honored Sunday by visiting nursing homes and by going to parks together. It was the one day they stopped everything and dedicated the day to God and family.

Things came to a head when Mary's travel volleyball team made it to the national championships, which took place during the days of the Easter Triduum: Good Friday, Holy Saturday, and Easter Sunday. Sister recalls,

> My team needed me. Since it was Holy Week, and my family wanted to be together, my whole family came to the tournament. We went to Holy Week services at a parish nearby. This time, though, it felt as though we were just checking it off the list to say we did it, and then we'd run back to the volleyball games. It felt horrible. The worst was Easter Sunday. I had two or three matches that day, on the holiest day of the year! I left during one match, changed into a dress, went to Easter Mass, and then raced back for my next game. Instead of being filled with Easter joy, I felt sick to my stomach. There was such a contrast between the heavenly meaning of the day, and the ultimately meaningless volleyball tournament. It turns out we all felt the same way, and I remember my mom saying that she regretted it and that we'd never do it again.

Was it sinful? It doesn't seem so. But they were not the type of people who settled—especially when it came to God. They lived the saying, "Give God what's right, not what's left."

It wasn't always like that. "We kept the moral life, but in a way, it was without heart, without the love behind it," Sister Mariana says. That changed when daughter Kathleen went on a youth retreat at Franciscan University of Steubenville. Her heart caught fire, and like the Olympic torchbearer, she brought it home. "We all grew in our desire for a personal relationship with God," Sister Mariana tells me. "Love for him became the reason behind the way we were living."

After Kathleen's retreat, Ann helped organize twenty-four-hour adoration at their church. If she couldn't find enough adorers, she'd send the kids.

The Divine Mercy chaplet was also a family favorite. A drive by their house might reveal the family kneeling before the images of the Sacred Heart and Our Lady of Guadalupe. The dog—an Australian Shepherd—was in on it, too. Maybe like the Little Match Girl in the fable, you would have stopped and looked through the window and imagined yourself there with them, sharing the warmth.

Sister Mariana says her parents would have gladly shared. Ann was always looking for the next person who needed help, and Kevin was a very affectionate and open man. She says, "He felt like he had a calling to be a Father to everybody. My friends would always love my dad. I was always sharing him with people." Sister doesn't remember her dad being angry, except if someone hurt his children, and she says her mom and dad *never fought*.

Mine didn't either. I always thought it wonderful. But Sister says there was a downside to it:

> I never learned to deal with conflict. No one ever told anyone else something was wrong. We didn't deal with problems. We didn't talk about it. We didn't know how to handle mistakes. To say, "It's okay. It's not the end of the world." When anything did happen, it was an explosion of stuff that had built up.

Sister confesses that it was she who did much of the exploding. "I was the troublemaker in the family. I was the one who would pick all the fights." She fought especially with her mother, Ann. When she was small, Sister recalls, "I never wanted to try anything new—swimming, piano, Girl Scouts. So my mom would make me, and then I would love it.

"I was in high school and my mom still had the mindset that she had to force me to do things. So when I wanted to stop playing basketball in tenth grade because it was stressful and I didn't enjoy it at all, she wouldn't believe me and tried everything to make me play," Sister explains.

Sometimes we moms have to learn to let go.

"When I started to babysit and get other little jobs, Mom had a hard time letting me go. We had so many emotional arguments." Finally Mary demanded to know why her mom was always getting in the way of her happiness. "It is because I want to spend time with you. It is because I love you," she answered.

"Wow—this knocked the wind out of me. I was amazed that my mom wanted to spend time with me. My frustration evaporated. It made me realize that my mom is a human being who needs to be loved and not just to be the one who is always giving and sacrificing. After that, my mom and I did grow really close," Sister Mariana recalls.

After high school, Mary entered Catholic University of America. It did not have a super-charged Catholic atmosphere, yet she was happy there. She met many fun and fervent Catholic friends. Even those who were not fervent acted differently (and better) when she was around—not that she went around correcting or criticizing her fellow students. "One of my weaknesses is that I'm a people pleaser," Sister says, "so I would never have made someone uncomfortable."

At the same time, the world didn't hold any attraction for her. "You just know where you are at home," she says. Home is what attracted Sister to her vocation as a Dominican teaching sister at Spiritus Sanctus Academy. She calls the place "a little piece of heaven": When you walk in the door, you immediately sense that this is a place of joy, a place of peace. You cannot miss the sign on the wall: "Be it known to all who enter here that Christ is the reason for this school." You are greeted warmly by the students dressed neatly in their uniforms with genuine smiles on their faces. The kids know that our number-one goal is "become a saint and go to heaven." This way of life is just like her home.

To this day, a sense of home goes with all the McGlynns wherever they are. Though scattered far and wide, they pray "together" daily. Each one renews the prayer they offered long ago when the Sacred Heart was enthroned in their home, the "Daily Renewal of Our Pledge of Love and Loyalty to Jesus, Our King, Provider, and Friend":

Dear Sacred Heart of Jesus, we renew our pledge of love and loyalty to you. Keep us always close to your loving heart and to the most pure heart of your Mother.

May we love one another more and more each day, forgiving each other's faults as you forgive us our sins. Teach us to see you in the members of our family and those we meet outside our home, and to love them as you love them, especially the poor and the oppressed, that we may be instrumental in bringing about justice and peace.

Please help us to carry our cross daily out of love for you, and to strengthen this love by frequent Mass and Communion.

Thank you, dear Jesus, King and Friend of our family, for all the blessings of this day. Protect us and all families during this night. Help us so to live that we may all get to heaven.

Immaculate Heart of Mary, pray for us!

St. Joseph, pray for us!

Our guardian angels, pray for us!

Saying Yes to the Greatest Commandment

I often think that my only shot at getting into heaven is if God grades on a curve. You know how it goes. I'm not a saint, but I'm not as bad as *some* people.

Maybe it's because when I was a kid my Mom told me that God gave us this life for a test. "Great," I remember thinking, "I am lousy at tests." Tests require that you don't daydream during class, that you don't use your little homework notebook for writing notes to pass to your friends, and that you don't wait and try to cram weeks of material into your head by singing it into the boiler.

My views on the hopelessness of tests changed in fifth grade when our class had a test that only the smart kids passed—barely. Our teaching sister realized that the test was too hard, so she graded us all on a curve. The smart kids got As and Bs. Some nameless people were just happy we passed. Finally, it paid to slack off!

Perhaps this was also how God operated. If life was a test, he had to know that it would be way too hard. Only the really amazing kids would pass. Once in a while an A student would come along, probably a martyr, and ace the test, but the vast sea of humanity wouldn't even know there was a test. At least *I* knew. I had even done some of the homework such as learning my catechism. If God graded on a curve, I might just squeak by.

I ask you, is this ringing a bell, clanging a gong, detonating a grenade in your ear? Is this not the way a lot of us think? Even as adults?

As we have seen, Sister Mariana's family once thought that way. "We kept the moral life, but in a way, it was without heart, without the love behind it." The school she attended was the same. She says, "We had Mass once a week, we had religion class, and we prayed at the end of the day. But the Faith and love for Jesus did not relate to the other activities of the day." It was love that changed all that. Sister's sister came home from her retreat on fire with the love of God.

Many people at this point will nod their heads and conclude that the rules don't matter. It's what is in the heart. But the McGlynns didn't throw out the rules. It was that all those "rules" now meant something.

Think of a relationship of lovers. Suppose one person in the couple remembers their wedding anniversary. The person clears the calendar, buys a gift, and plans a special dinner to celebrate the day. That's how a lover is supposed to act, right? Now suppose the other person in the relationship shows up distracted, eats in a hurry, then says, "Is it over? I have a game." Is that how a lover is supposed to act?

St. John Vianney didn't think so.

> But, you will say to me, who are these people who are partly on God's side and partly on the side of the world? These people look upon Sunday as merely a day for rest and amusement. They stay in bed longer than on weekdays, and instead of giving themselves to God with all their hearts, they do not even think of Him. Some of them will be thinking of their amusements, others of people they expect to meet, still others of the sales they are about to make or the money they will be spending or receiving. With great difficulty they will manage the Sign of the Cross in some fashion or another. Because they will be going to church later, they will omit their prayers altogether, saying: "Oh, I'll have plenty of time to say them before Mass." They always have something to do before setting out for Mass, and although they have been planning to say their prayers before setting out, they are barely in time for the beginning of the Mass itself.*

Ouch. If you'll excuse me, I'm off to Confession.

---

* The Work of God Apostolate, "Sermons of the Curs de Ars," Catholic Sermons, www.theworkofgod.org/Library/Sermons/JdVianey/Sermons.htm#THEY ARE FOR THE WORLD (accessed May 29, 2013).

Sunday is the day Christ united us to himself, rising from the dead and completing our redemption, giving us his very own life in the food of Holy Communion. What is our attitude to this infinite love?

The McGlynns wanted to show God that this anniversary meant something to them. It would seem that they went above and beyond the actual obligations about Sunday. Then again, Jesus said that the greatest commandment was to love God with your whole heart, soul, mind and strength. Not exactly a minimalist approach, is it?

Ten More
Like You

Saying Yes to Generosity

Father Jeremy Paulin, O.M.V.

Pray and work.

The last time I saw Jeremy Paulin I was trying to get rid of him. No, he wasn't an unwanted suitor or a salesman. He was a squatter in my domicile.

Actually, it wasn't mine, and that is just the point. It belonged to the Christian Brothers, members of the

teaching order founded by St. Jean Baptist de LaSalle.
Greg as a graduate student found lodgings with them at
their boarding house for high school boys in Feldkirch,
Austria. After we were married, they generously let me
move in, too.

However, the brothers did not consider the arrange-
ment permanent. We were already on notice to find something more suitable than the two-room infirmary with
bath and toilet that they provided. This was, after all, a
guys' dorm, and I was the wrong kind. What's more, we
paid pauper's rent. I tried to repay them by watering the
plants, which they more or less put up with. They were
happier with Greg, who took an interest in our fellow
boarders, guys under the age of twenty, who were away
from home and could get wild if the mood struck them—
which it did as punctually as a German clock. He brought
them along with us to Mass, warned them against sneak-
ing the local *Fräuleins* up to their rooms, and invited them
in for frequent suppers of fried garlic and noodles, cooked
on our two-burner hot plate. (Maybe he figured if the
advice didn't keep the girls away, the garlic and noodles
would.) Still, we knew we were charity cases and were
careful to stay in the brothers' good graces.

We had started to ease off on the apartment hunting
because I had discovered I was *mit Kind*—with child. I
had also discovered that the word *schwanger*—pregnant—
was *verboten*. My gentle, elderly confessor in town, a holy
Jesuit with impeccable English, winced when I used it. He
said it wasn't properly human. It was bovine.

At that point, I felt more bovine than human. For one
thing, I was off my cud. Garlic and noodles wasn't about
to stay where I put it anyway. Visits from the guys were

becoming less welcome, too. I just wanted to sit alone in my stall, chew on some dry grass, and moo.

That's when Jeremy showed up unannounced, and worse, unalone.

He was once a schoolmate of mine at Thomas More, a small, classical, liberal arts college, and he was now dedicating himself to bumming around Europe with two fellow delinquents. The three of them paid their way as "buskers." Jeremy, off for the winter from his Massachusetts construction job, and his buddy, a classical pianist, played accordion on the street. The third member re-created Renaissance and Baroque masterpieces on the sidewalk. Oh sure, they sound cool *now*. One of them knew of the *Heim*, our dormitory, and led his companions straight to the downstairs lounge.

I found them with the TV on and their feet up. Great. Next thing, they'd be rummaging through the fridge looking for beer. My one thought was, "If I don't kick them out fast, the brothers will. But how?"

Then I spotted it. There, bathed in golden light, was my savior. Okay, it was only a bus schedule on a table under a lamp. But it was all I needed.

Twenty-two years later, I wish I had saved one, just to show my children that once upon a time I really could do higher math. The bus schedule was a small, thin, white piece of paper, covered in tiny black symbols, forming a grid pattern. Learning how to decipher one of those things was a rare accomplishment—one reserved for residents. The guys lounging before me may have gone from city to city and seen more of Europe's treasures than I ever would, but I—I knew how to read the local bus schedule.

I showed it to Jeremy and waited for his eyes to cross. I then explained that the last bus out of town was leaving in about nine minutes. It would take them at least six to hoof it to the bus stop. What I meant by "the last bus" was, of course, "the last bus until the one after that." This was not an outright lie but a classic mental reservation. This device is covered in every respectable catechism and is deemed thoroughly Catholic in times of emergency, such as if the Gestapo is banging on your door or if vagrants are hanging around in your apartment building. As hoped, the guys took "last bus" to mean, "last bus of the evening" or perhaps even "last bus for the next six weeks." With no beer in sight anyway, it was a quick goodbye. They were gone before the brothers could detect that the TV had even been warm.

It's been my dirty little secret for twenty-two years. I didn't confess it until the day I Facebooked (this is a verb now) Jeremy—who now has the venerable title "Father" before his name—to ask him if he'd like to take part in my vocations book. As vocation director for the O.M.V.s, the Oblates of the Virgin Mary, in Boston, Massachusetts, he said yes. "Anything to encourage future vocations."

Hmmm . . . Anything? I suspect he remembered that I was not generous with the beer.

✳

Father Jeremy Paulin's Facebook profile reveals a long list of those who have come before him, those who made it possible for him to be a priest:

> I was ordained a priest November 6, 2006, by: Bishop Alexander Salazar (2004), Roger Michael Cardinal Mahony (1975), Bishop Hugh Aloysius Donohue + (1947), Archbishop John Joseph Mitty +

(1926), Patrick Joseph Cardinal Hayes + (1914), John
Murphy Cardinal Farley + (1895) . . .

On the list went down to Scipione Cardinal Rebiba
year of ordination, 15 something-something. Unless
Rebiba went to heaven in a fiery chariot, he too is probably +. I was really hoping to see Peter + (33) listed, with
Jesus + (temporarily) then ^ (1) at the start of it. But the
records preceding the sixteenth century seem to be lost.
(I blame feudal wars and the Black Death personally.)

The episcopal lineage is not the only lineage of a
priest, as Bishop Alexander Salazar, who ordained Father
Jeremy, acknowledged. In his homily at the ordination
Mass, he thanked the new priest's family in Massachusetts for being his "first seminary." It was there that Father
learned generosity first.

Clarence and Elizabeth Paulin began by being generous with God. They had ten children—all of whom
happen to have names that start with J. "Mom and Dad
weren't super well off," Father tells me. Coming from a
family of eight kids, I kind of guessed that.

To provide for the numerous J's, both parents had
incomes. "Dad climbed utility poles, and Mom worked
as an RN in between having children." He told me that
the hospital was conveniently located five minutes away.
With utility poles, an RN job, ten births, and all the twisted
ankles and broken elbows a big family could wish for, he
says "convenient" with a straight face.

As soon as each of the ten J's was of age, Mom and
Dad required them to follow in their footsteps and get
jobs. They wanted them to be responsible with money.
So, Jeremy and his siblings got paper routes. After that,
at the ripe age of fourteen, Jeremy got a summer job as
a Connecticut shade tobacco picker, rising early in the

morning to catch a bus to work at a job that paid less than minimum wage. Later he climbed the economic ladder by busing tables and washing dishes.

There were chores around the house and yard as well—a garden and chickens to tend, grass to mow, and a long driveway to shovel in the winter. I find myself nodding as he describes his childhood, something like mine except for the chickens, tobacco, and fixation on J names. I could probably sketch the garage—the boxes of dusty potatoes, the bruised apples ready for the cider press, the rusty shovels and mowers side by side ready to be called into action—a garage full of everything a hard-working family needs—except the car, which must give up its lodgings and live outside.

It was this formation in hard work that influenced Father Jeremy in his work as a vocation director for the oblates. According to Father Jeremy, one of the key qualities of a promising candidate is a strong work ethic. Another important attribute is an affirmative answer to the question, "Can this man make a commitment?"

A commitment—Jeremy's parents made a commitment to one another, one which they made at their marriage and renewed again and again throughout their married life of almost sixty years. The most radical commitment came in 1979, when they had a conversion of sorts. It led them to change their family culture almost overnight.

Some of their children had started to lapse in the Faith. Jeremy's mom and dad didn't wait around to see if the problem would go away on its own. It was like spiritual cancer. Find the cause; find the treatment—no delay. Pray and work.

The local public school was deemed a bad influence. So Dad "yanked the kids out." He enrolled all but the youngest, who would be homeschooled, in small schools run by sisters and lay men and women.

This news was greeted by "ranting, raving, and cussing" from Jeremy. He had friends. He fit in. This new school was for dorks. Dad was too busy selling the TV to listen. "He sold it for a dollar—to one of my friends!"

Then they started praying the Rosary. You know, the prayer of little old ladies with thick foreign accents. It's really the prayer that Our Lady herself recommends to every Catholic to strengthen virtue, combat sin, and even convert the world. All that for fifteen minutes a day? God is generous. Mom and Dad sneaked it in, just for Lent. Oh, sure—I know the type. My parents were the same way. Before you could blink, they had you on your knees nightly and were tacking all these extra prayers on at the end. They even did it when, you know, *people* were around. They had no shame.

One time, a Protestant friend of Jeremy's was visiting when somebody announced that it was time to pray the Rosary. Jeremy was mortified. Then the friend asked if he could join in. Maybe Mom and Dad were onto something.

To ease the transition to the dorky new school, Jeremy's parents introduced their children to the other families during the summer. It was then that he realized he was among his own kind. They didn't have TV either. It felt good to think, "We're not the only ones." Translation: "Maybe we're not weird after all. Okay, we're weird, but we aren't alone." He fit in and the friends he made there he keeps to this day.

Making tuition payments meant taking out a second mortgage. An even bigger problem was fitting the demands of the new schools into their busy schedules. Mom got up early and drove sixty miles round trip to and from the school every morning. Then she went to work. Meanwhile, she was taking courses to complete her bachelor's degree in nursing. At the end of the day, she hit the trail again and picked the kids up—two hundred miles a day total. I certainly hope her guardian angel had supper on the table when she got home. "I can never repay my parents," says Father Jeremy. "They not only sacrificed; they never resented it." His mom often says, "We wish we had ten more just like you."

The fruit of that ready sacrifice was that Jeremy learned to pray. At school, and later when I knew him in college, he went out of his way to pray and get closer to God.

His vocation to the priesthood first showed itself then, in a still, small voice. He first met the oblates back in college, but a teacher encouraged him to complete his studies before entering. After college, Jeremy got an apartment with some guys, started a construction company, and slowly, without realizing it, left off praying. He kept the minimum—Sunday Mass, the Rosary, weekly confession (well, what he calls the minimum anyway). But there was no longer that quiet time given to meditation, the kind of prayer that "enlarges the heart" and makes it possible to hear the whispering of the Holy Spirit.

It was during those years that I saw him in Europe. He looked to me like a guy who was just wasting time being a bachelor. What do I know? As Jeremy worked his way through Europe, he visited the shrines—among them Beauraing, Knock, Einsiedeln, and Lourdes. These experiences helped him a few years later in a new venture—organizing and directing pilgrimages. As he led pilgrims around the now-familiar cities and shrines and led them in the Rosary, a number of them suggested he'd make a good priest. On one of these pilgrimages—to Lourdes—a priest said, "Everyone is here for a reason." Jeremy, ever the worker, thought, "That's right. I'm here because I work here." But these pilgrimages were leading him back to his calling.

While praying the old, familiar Rosary in the upper basilica at Lourdes, Our Lady let him know she was there and that he was where he should be. I sense embarrassment in his voice when he tells me it made him cry. He quickly follows it up with, "I don't know why. I didn't understand it. I still don't fully. It was what it was."

The signs were like puzzle pieces coming together to form a complete picture. People on pilgrimage thought he should be a priest. Back home his mom told him he'd make a good father. How did the two fit together? At Mass, God weighed in. The words of the Mass stood out. He had an inner feeling that God was asking him to *pray* those words, the words which only the priest says. This time when he heard the calling, he proved himself his parents' son—there was no delay.

His father ran a pilgrimage yearly to the shrine of St. Anne de Beaupre in Canada, to pray for our nation in its fight to protect the unborn. Jeremy decided to go on that pilgrimage, not as a leader, but as a pilgrim. His intention was to discern his vocation. He told no one. There, two older ladies approached him and told him he had the look of a seminarian about him. It's not necessarily mystical. If you hang out in Catholic churches all your life, you can spot one. They had him pegged.

On his return, the bus stopped at a McDonald's in White River Junction, Vermont. Inside was a man in a black suit and Roman collar. Jeremy went up and greeted

him respectfully as "Father." "I'm not a priest yet," the
man said. "I'm a seminarian from the Oblates of the Virgin Mary in Boston."

The Oblates of the Virgin Mary? Oh, yes. It was like
seeing the girl next door after a long absence and finding
out she'd grown up and had been waiting for you all the
while.

The Oblates is just the sort of place in which you'd
expect him to be at home after a lifetime formation from
Mom and Dad in work at the service of prayer. It is an
active order that works to form diocesan priests and lay
men and women in the spirituality of St. Ignatius. Some
of these people are then equipped to become spiritual
directors themselves.

That day in my apartment building, all I saw were
three guys disguised as vagrants. Father told me that one
became a lawyer and the other a psychologist. The third
became an *alter Christus*. Who knew?

Saying Yes to Generosity

The fifth chapter in *The Rule of St. Benedict* tells the monk
to work cheerfully, with a generous heart. Only then will
the deed "be acceptable to God and agreeable to men." Do
what is required "without hesitation, delay, lukewarm-
ness, grumbling or complaint." He left out, "massaging
your pitiful, little ego." It's not enough to do the work.
You are supposed to do it with a generous spirit.

Grumbling and whining, like illicit love affairs, feel
so right at first. Then the bloom of self-consolation fades
away, and you discover that you've been nurturing a
weed. Its roots penetrate deep down into your conception
of yourself and what you think you deserve. By the time

you find out you've got one of these weeds, it has grown huge and prickly and has dug in deep. Good luck pulling that thing out. You've really got to get down in the dirt and dig out the whole thing at once or it will grow back. How do I know? Don't ask.

How could I relate to Father's parents, who worked so hard that I get tired just reading about it? Don't they seem a bit like those saints written about long ago, who were born fasting? I don't know about you, but I automatically separate those saints out in my mind as more angelic than human. I can't relate. Therefore, I can't imitate. Please, Lord, hold me excused.

You have to read between the lines to find out about his parents' interior struggles. "We wish we had ten more kids just like you." What is Mrs. Paulin, the bionic woman? No. She's at the point in her life now when she can look back on all the work, all the fatigue, all the sacrifice, and tell her family how worth it they were to her—so worth it that she'd do double duty if she could. That encourages me to keep on going. She seems to be saying that the Christian life is not a "just add salvation" recipe. Grace is in the daily renewal of purpose.

Mrs. Paulin seems to have gotten her wish and more in spiritual grandchildren. Priests always have spiritual children. She did not get just ten more, but hundreds. And each of those have their own hundreds of spiritual children. And on down it goes just like the episcopal lineage.

God is never outdone in generosity.

Doctor of
Souls

Saying Yes to Humility

Father Bernard Ezaki,
Diocese of Allentown, Pennsylvania

**Ask God to give me
something better.**

One Sunday afternoon, Father Bernard Ezaki heard a knock at the rectory door. "I immediately thought of Stonewall Jackson," he says. (Wouldn't anybody?) He explains, "Stonewall was interested in Catholicism, so he knocked on a rectory door, but no one answered. He went away. I figured I'd better open the door."

It wasn't the ghost of old Stonewall seeking to be shriven. It was just some lady Father Bernard had never seen before. She told him she was a baptized Catholic but had been going to a Protestant church. She didn't feel right there. Among other things, her minister didn't believe in angels. Father talked to her awhile. The following Easter, she came back into the Church.

Wow! That was easy. Father is a patient and able apologist. But before he even got started, this lady was ready to listen. She had gone to the rectory dressed—as a sort of a test—"as seductively as possible." If the priest dared to say anything against it, she would say, "Fine. If I'm not dressed good enough for you then I'm not good enough for your God!"

So who answers the door? A blind priest. "It was God giving her a kick in the pants," Father laughs. He loves a good joke. This is one of his favorite stories about how God took his sight to give him something better.

You will pardon me, but the deal seems a bit unfair. Being nearly blind from birth (he gets a little help from a magnifying glass) is not my idea of one of life's golden gifts. If God were to hand it to me, I'd keep the receipt and try to exchange it when he wasn't looking.

I've been wearing eyewear by Magoo since I was twelve. I have the gift of clumsiness to match. I routinely walk into walls and sharp corners and once even shot my entire body up headfirst like the Saturn V into the pantry door frame, while trying to get noodles down from the top shelf. So far, this has converted no one, and I certainly never thought of it as a gift.

It's a good thing Father is not like me. He's not like anyone I know. For one thing, I don't know any other Japanese-Slovak Americans who go around pretending to be Irish. That's Father's way of handling delicate conversations. His maxim: "You can say anything you want in an Irish accent." Okay, then he won't mind if I say, "Faith and Begorrah! How did a nice Catholic girl like your mother wind up married to a Buddhist?"

Mary and Toshio met during World War II. The Japanese had not yet won our hearts with the Toyota. They were loathed and feared—which was sort of the mood they were going for when they bombed Pearl Harbor and so on. But it was rather hard on Japanese-Americans. They were mistrusted so much that they were forced out of their homes in California and sent to live in camps. Father's dad had just finished medical school in Philadelphia when his parents in California were ordered to abandon their property and report to a camp in the rural West somewhere. He didn't dare go back to California.

The newly qualified Dr. Ezaki tried to get a job at one Catholic hospital in Philadelphia, but he was turned down. He then found work in a hospital run by German nuns. (Maybe they knew what it was like.) It was there that he met Mary, a novice.

Wait, wait, wait. Back up! She was a nun? Well, sort of—she hadn't yet made final vows.

They had what was commonly called a "mixed marriage." The Church didn't outright forbid such marriages between two people of separate religions, but in the 1950s the Church did her utmost to discourage them. The reason was that the Catholic spouse's faith and the faith of any future children could be in danger. No human relationship could be more important than one's relationship

with God. However, if the Catholic spouse was deter-
mined to go ahead, the marriage could proceed—as long
as the non-Catholic promised to raise the kids Catholic.
(Today, the vow is just that the non-Catholic won't *inter-
fere* with a Catholic upbringing.) And just to make sure
everyone got the message that marrying a non-Catholic
was unwise, there could be no nuptial Mass in the church
proper. The vows took place outside the sanctuary before
a small party of witnesses.

I can imagine readers bristling from coast to coast.
"Why don't they just name the first-born child 'Anathema'
while they're at it?" These rules of the Church seem an
affront against personal rights, freedom, and equality.
You'd think that with a heritage such as that, Father himself would be bristling over it, decades later. But again,
he's not like most people. To Father (and all Catholics),
marriage is not a path through this life only; it's a path to
heaven. It is a vocation every bit as serious as his priesthood. For parents to be of one mind about God sure helps.
"Tell everyone," he commands me, "that the role of the
father in validating the Faith is indispensible." If you are
still bristling, read it again in an Irish accent. He says it
helps.

Dr. and Mrs. Ezaki had a loving and lasting marriage.
"Dad would never leave home without kissing Mom
goodbye," Father says. "I never heard my parents argu-
ing. I never heard my father raise his voice to my mother."

Dr. Ezaki enjoyed talking to the priests and sisters
Mrs. Ezaki often invited over. They were educated, and he
prized education as the one thing no one could take from
a person. Yet, Mrs. Ezaki told her son that it was hard not
being able to share the Faith with her husband. While
Father's dad was never anti-Catholic, he rarely went to

church himself. He unintentionally gave his children the impression that faith wasn't necessary. "If he'd been a bad guy, it might have been different. They could blame it on him not being Catholic. But he was a good guy. So they say, Dad didn't need it," Father Bernard explains.

Dr. Ezaki was more than a good guy. He was a wise and honorable man, not to mention a gifted surgeon—all seemingly without the Church. I say "seemingly" because when your devout wife is on her knees daily for you, you're really not on your own.

Out of six children, Bernard was the only one who kept the Faith. You might wonder why he did. He will tell you frankly that part of the reason was that while his five siblings went to the local Catholic school, only the public school had the resources to teach the blind. So that's where he went. This is another case where his blindness served to his advantage. To make religion feel more "relevant," the local Catholic school was trying no end of weird things.

Father gives no details, but here's an example from my own childhood, more or less in that era: My Confirmation retreat master stripped off all his clothes—except for something like tights—and put on a clown suit, wig, and red nose. He then went around the room tickling our noses with a feather duster, handing out candy, and telling us God loved us. It's hard to take the Faith seriously under those conditions.

It was in public school that a young Bernard learned to take God seriously. It was Mrs. Hastler, "a grand Protestant lady," he says in his stage brogue. "She talked to our fifth-grade class about how the Communists wouldn't let people worship God. 'Boys and girls,' she said, 'go to church every week.' I remember praying, 'God, if you are

real, like Mrs. Hastler says, I want to know you.'" May
she be richly rewarded.

At home, Father's mother formed him in the expression of his faith and in his imagination. "She gave me my
faith, my name Bernard after a visit to Lourdes, and all
the culture I happen to have—a love of Gilbert and Sul-
livan, the children's opera *Hansel and Gretel*, *The Sound of
Music*, *High Society*, *The Scarlet and the Black*, and *My Fair
Lady*." His mother formed his imagination in the simplest,
oldest, most venerable way—by reading aloud to him.
She chose books that went beyond mere entertainment:

> But for them it was only the beginning of the real
> story. All their life in this world and all their adven-
> tures in Narnia had only been the cover and the title
> page: now at last they were beginning Chapter One
> of the Great Story which no one on earth has read:
> which goes on forever: in which every chapter is bet-
> ter than the one before. (C. S. Lewis, *The Last Battle*)

That is not all. In reading aloud you have a giver and
a receiver. One reads; the other responds. Did you ever
read aloud to your kids and then hear them reading the
same thing aloud to their younger brothers and sisters?
They are using your emphasis. They are hearing your
voice. They not only love the words that you love, they
are loving you through the words. In this way, Mary Ezaki
formed her son's heart and his future priesthood. "I think
my mom made me a romantic," he says. "I tend to favor
the image of Christ as a Bridegroom."

Father Ezaki writes about it in an allegorical fairy
tale, "The Courtship of Esmeralda." A beautiful, hard-
hearted princess marries a lover whom she has never
seen. It will be a full year before he will keep his pledge
and reveal himself to her. She fears he is a monster. But

when he comes to her at night, she is entranced by his presence. Night after night, her love for him grows. The day approaches and a new fear takes the place of the old. Now she is not afraid to see his face—she is afraid he will see hers. She confesses her unworthiness to him. But he assures her that his love is unchanging. And the more she experiences his love, the more beautiful she will become. This is a story of the Holy Eucharist, coming hidden to the faithful soul.

Dr. Ezaki also gave Bernard an enviable formation in words. In an essay called "The Surgeon's Tongue," Father writes movingly about the lessons his dad taught him. He gave Bernard the Japanese name *Ichiban*, meaning "Number-One Son." In Japanese custom, it denotes birth order and inheritance, but to Bernard it was more. It expressed love and honor, and he strove to be worthy of it.

The power of a name was a lesson he has taken into his pastoral work and into his work as a high school religion teacher. For a time he called his students *Kinderschweine*—child pigs—because of the way they messed up the classroom. He thought it was funny and hoped it would induce them to be neater. It did not. After a friend expressed horror at the nickname, Father took a different approach. He decided to address each student with the Japanese suffix *san*, which means "honorable." (Brittney-san and Trevor-san—right.) Guess what? They began to act honorably. The classroom stayed cleaner, too.

Dr. Ezaki was careful about the words he used to discipline his children. Father says it was a lot like the way he did surgery—steadily and cleanly, with no put-downs or abusive language. With disease, he was a destroyer. With the patient, he was as gentle as a Zen garden. He never lost sight of the goal, whether it was the well-being of the patient or the well-being of one of his children.

Father himself, as seen in the *Kinderschweine* episode, had to mess this up before he got it right with his students. There was the time a kid threw a wad of paper across the room. Father Bernard explains:

"How dare this brat take unfair advantage of my blindness!" I thought to myself. "I'll fix his wagon!" I perceived the young man's offense as a personal affront, and I was going to get even. That night, I plotted as to how I would make him pay for his blatant disrespect. The next day, in front of his peers, I thoroughly humiliated the boy by forcing him to sweep the floor after I had angrily dumped out the contents of the trash can. I did this, not once, but three times!

The next paper the student handed in had these words written very small across the bottom, "I am a failure." It was an eye opener. "I was more blind than I knew."

Luckily, seeing his father practice medicine taught Father Ezaki how to repair a wound. "Sew up the incision with small stitches so as not to leave a scar." That was also how his dad handled him. Dad may have raised his voice, he may have laid down the law, he may even have lost his cool, but afterward he made a point of showing the child there was no grudge, with a smile, a compliment, or an act of friendliness. Father now follows up classroom discipline the same way. When he must correct a student legitimately, he follows it up with praise and encouragement. The goal is the well-being of the student.

Years after his death, Dr. Ezaki's patients still tell Father what a great healer Dr. Ezaki was. Father Ezaki may not know it, but he too has that reputation—and not simply because he shares Christ's power to forgive sins. It's a personal trait.

I recognized it long ago. A neighbor asked me for the name of a priest who could help her friend go to confession after an abortion. His was the name I thought of first. Over the years, for delicate matters, I have often referred people to him. The blind guy with the stage Irish, he puts everybody at ease.

Well, almost everybody. An elderly friend of Greg's, named John, was finally at his end. A high-church Episcopalian, John had always enjoyed talking to Greg about the sacraments. As time went on, he began to express a desire to become Catholic. There was only one thing stopping him—his beloved wife, Mary. All talk of Catholicism was hushed up whenever she was around. But now it was getting crucial. Only a few sands were left in the hourglass, and John had made it clear that he wanted the sacraments before he died. Greg came to me. Who could we bring over there who would put Mary at her ease? I had the brilliant idea to get the ever-gentle, ever-amiable Father Ezaki.

He walked into the hospital room talking like the leprechaun on the Lucky Charms box, "I'm here to be helpin' John prepare for his death." His greeting was returned by silence—stony silence—from Mary. He didn't need his magnifying glass to tell him there was a hairy eyeball trained on him, and it was set on "kill." Greg finally broke the tension and suggested, "I'm not sure Father *O'Flanahan* is what we want here." Father instantly morphed back into his American self. He talked to Mary in terms she could understand. Then, with her blessing, he took care of John.

After John's confession, Father looked at him lying in his hospital bed, unable to move, ravaged by Parkinson's with just days left to live, and said to my husband, "Gee, I'd love to be him, right now." Did I mention Father Ezaki's not like most people?

I don't know anyone like him for the capacity to heal. With good eyesight he might have followed in his father's footsteps. But God wanted him for something better. "I think of myself as a doctor of souls when I hear confession." His father's lessons and spirit are never far from him. "I often picture my father watching me and nodding while I shrive."

There is a diversity of gifts in the kingdom of God, says St. Paul in 1 Corinthians. To some is given knowledge, to some miracles, to others prophecy. Now, in this age of broken hearts, father's gift is healing. In a world marred by spiritual blindness, here is one who sees, not with keen eyesight, but with keen insight. He asked me once to pray for him before a cataract operation. "If God takes what is left of my sight," he said, "ask him to give me something better." It struck me that this is how we are all supposed to pray—not to ask for the gifts we want but for the higher gifts that God knows we need.

It was Toshio Ezaki who sensed that his number-one son was given much more than was taken away when he lost his sight at birth, and that it was all to some higher purpose. Says Father, "I distinctly remember him saying that I would play a key part in the well-being of our family. I wanted, and still want, to live up to his lofty opinion of me." This special mission would begin when Father Ezaki, possessing the faith of his mother and the grace of the priesthood, escorted his noble father late in his life to the baptismal font and became his godfather.

Saying Yes to Humility

There are times (especially when estrogen is at low tide) when the whole, comprehensive task of forming children in heart, mind, and body looms before me frighteningly, like a steep, craggy mountain I've got to climb—in slippers . . . and I've forgotten to eat breakfast.

Mothers are not allowed to be weak. Whoever invented the term "weaker sex" didn't know any mothers. Our husbands don't believe it, or they wouldn't come up to us when we're collapsed on the couch and ask if we know where the duct tape is. Our kids certainly don't believe it, or they wouldn't ask us if we want to jump on the trampoline with them. We don't believe it either. We get up and find the duct tape and after that go jump on the trampoline, because if we don't, we feel we're slacking.

Yet, mothers do not have limitless energy. We become exhausted—emotionally more than physically. We often work through our fatigue because everyone depends on Mom. This seems as if it's a good idea until we find ourselves playing the part of the green-faced witch from *The Wizard of Oz*.

On the night Father Ezaki came over to have the image of the Sacred Heart enthroned in our home, I felt like a slacker. The Sacred Heart kit had collected dust for a solid ten years—I found it when we moved. The dinner I made that evening didn't quite turn out. It was embarrassing. All I lacked was the flour-sack dress, the curlers, and the stockings rolled down around my ankles.

Father ate the food without complaining. He led the service. Afterward he stopped and told the kids he had a secret to tell them: "Every night when I go to sleep, I pray that Jesus will make my heart like his. I ask him to give me open-heart surgery—to take out my heart and put his in its place. But it has to be while I'm sleeping because I'm too weak to stand it while I'm awake." And I knew he understood. He understood, not just the feeling of weakness, but the feeling of mortified pride that often goes with it.

Sometimes God holds our limitations before our eyes—not to beat us down and remind us that we are lower than worms—but to let us know that those limitations aren't going to stop him. They are his glory. And they can be ours, if we accept them. It will be those very limitations that he will use to transform our hearts from stone to flesh.

The Humble Excavating and Cinderblock Work

Saying Yes to Patience

Sister Chiara Marie of Jesus, True Light, P.C.P.A., and
Sister Marie St. Francis of the Crucified One, P.C.P.A.

> **This is what I want
> my family to be like.**

When you see a happy family, you might think they've
always had it made. Sister Chiara Marie and Sister Marie
St. Francis (formerly Regina and Genevieve Cunningham)
grew up in such a family.

Sister Chiara tells the story for both sisters, since at the time of our interview Sister Marie St. Francis was in her canonical year, a period of withdrawal from the world.

Sister Chiara has dark, curly hair and smiling, dark eyes. She looks like her dad, Bill. Sister Marie St. Francis takes after her mother, Cecilia, with fair hair and large, light eyes.

We've known their family for years. In many ways, our lives are parallel. Greg and Bill rowed together at La Salle College in Philadelphia. By coincidence, Cecilia and I were schoolmates in college in New Hampshire. Our numerous homeschooled kids did not grow up together, but they've always clicked when they have met—laughing and talking as if they've known each other all their lives.

Anyone looking on would guess that Bill and Cecilia themselves were, like Greg and I, from happy homes. Looking at their happy kids, you'd never know how much they had to overcome. Cecilia tells me that Bill grew up without his father. Later, he suffered the loss of his relationship with his stepfather as well, to divorce. Cecilia's family was racked by generations of mental illness and alcoholism. The results in her generation included drugs, crime, depression, and suicide.

Growing up, the one warm light in Cecilia's house was her sister Jeannie, who took a mother's care of her while their mom worked to provide. "When we changed the sheets, she would put the fitted sheet on and let me lie down on it and make the bed around me," Cecilia says. "I'd be asleep before she was done. To this day she's my best friend." It was Jeannie who put their sorrows into words echoing scripture: the sins of the fathers are visited upon the children.

How, then, did it come to be that the Cunningham family turned out so different—that their nine children have known none of this pain? Bill and Cecilia resolved that the cycle of destruction would end with them.

Sister Chiara tells me that this thought first entered her mom's heart when her mom was only eight or nine. She was sitting in church behind a young family when the toddler tripped on the kneeler and hurt himself. His older brother reached down and picked him up. As he hugged him and kissed him, Cecilia was struck by the thought, "That's what I want my family to be like."

It was the first stirring of her maternity—grace awakening in her. Cecilia says, "I firmly believe that God took my desire as a prayer and granted it."

The Holy Spirit is a strange bird—a master of pulling the mystical out of the ordinary moment. He touched Bill similarly once, under his other guise, the wind. Bill told me the story once, while sitting at my kitchen table. He was walking on the grounds of the Shrine of Our Lady of Czestochowa when he saw a girl walking in the distance on a windy hillside. Her long, brown hair was loose and blowing in the wind. Her full skirt was billowing. "Who is that?" he remembers thinking. She seemed like a vision to him. It was Cecilia, age nineteen. Later, they both happened to belong to the same choir at the shrine. The priest switched songbooks on them so they'd have to meet. (The Holy Spirit sometimes works with an accomplice.)

Bill's devotion would win Cecilia's heart. Knowing the tragedy of divorce in his own life, he told her, "The *d* word will never pass our lips."

Their first home wasn't glamorous, just a tiny, one-bedroom apartment over a garage. The amenities were a clothesline and a garden, both of which Cecilia loved. The entrance was up a flight of concrete steps on the outside of the building. She would trudge up those steps often, in the glare of the summer sun, hauling groceries, pregnant out to the next county with son Joseph. On a bad day, she would *crawl* up because of a blood-sugar crash, having waited too long to eat.

Not too many months after Joseph was born, she found herself trudging or crawling up the blinding-white steps, groceries in one arm, Joseph in the other, pregnant out to the next county—again. This was Genevieve.

It was tough to be homebound with children so small. But it could be even tougher to take them out. Cecilia tells me about the time she dressed Joseph and Genevieve up in holiday finery for Bill's office Christmas party. Normally the sight of a boy and girl brings smiles from strangers—"the perfect family." But by then Regina was on the way, and three's a crowd. People on the elevator sneered and said, "Are they *all* yours?" Cecilia's hand went protectively to her belly. "Nope. This one's adopted."

She was well stocked with one-liners. Her sense of humor came in handy through the years of raising young children. There would be six more, nine in all. The others have names—John Paul, Stephen, Liam, Caeli, Miriam, and Gianna. But sometimes people would just stand there pointing and counting them. Some mentioned "responsibility" and "prevention."

And what about overpopulation? The Cunninghams had outgrown houses and cars and had once maxed out at eight people to one bathroom. Yup, they understood overpopulation.

Those were the years of sacrifice. Bill worked on commission selling life insurance. Sales demanded a lot of time on the road, and money was often tight. Cecilia admits that their money struggles sometimes got to her. "So many times, I felt irresponsible for having another baby. It's hard to be a witness to the cynics when you yourself feel such doubt."

For the first ten years living in the suburbs of Philadelphia, she had a Rosary group that kept her going. She says,

> The other moms and I met weekly and prayed with twenty to thirty kids running all over the place. We laughed together over tea after prayers. We cried together in our sorrows, we prayed each other through some real crosses. Those years prepared me for the later times, when I was truly alone in our various trials.

The "alone" part kicked in when Bill changed careers. For the next ten years they relocated every one to two years. The frequent moves meant never really settling down. The hardest part was that sometimes the family lived far away from other Catholics. Other times, they didn't stay long enough in one place to make close friendships.

Meanwhile, that feeling of not fitting in came and went. When living in mainline Philadelphia they felt like the Beverly Hillbillies, riding around town in their huge van. When they moved to the Bible Belt, the van was no problem. But the fact that its name was "Ave" was. They were those dreaded Catholics. "It was brutal," Cecilia recalls. "But that's not what I think of first. I remember the joy."

She shared her love of the outdoors with the kids. As a girl, she used to explore the woods and fields around her home. Now, nature became her kids' playground, too.

She took them on walks, pointing out the wildflowers, the birds, and the horses in their pastures.

"With Dad it was boats," says Sister Chiara. Bill would take the kids rowing on the Schuylkill River. Sister Chiara remembers being charmed by a purple boat with a Tweety Bird decal on it. They'd drive in his old haunts down Kelly Drive, in Philadelphia, past the statues along the sunny, green expanse on the banks: the Pony Express, the Viking, Jack Kelly—Grace Kelly's father, an Olympic champion rower. Their destination was Boat House Row. At night, the boathouses would shine with lights, their outlines reflected in the shimmering water.

Those outings with Mom and Dad bonded the family. Their closeness was meant to go with them wherever they went. If Bill heard that one of the kids was picked on or left out at the playground or ball field, he would ask the others point blank, "What did you do about it?" They could more easily tell him they got arrested for disorderly conduct than say they stood by and did nothing.

Cecilia grew close to her kids through homeschooling. She had planned to do it well before she ever had children. Sister says that they called her "Pioneer Mom" because she was the first in her group of friends to try it. She took hope from the real pioneers who did so much with so little.

Cecilia homeschooled through morning sickness and exhaustion, sometimes teaching from the couch.

She prayed daily with the kids, but there was nothing Zen about it. Her older kids remember her shouting, "Shut *up*! It's time to pray!" She often worried that her prayer and catechism weren't structured and regular enough. "It seemed so little at the time compared to what others were doing." Some homeschoolers attend 7 a.m.

Mass every day, never miss a Rosary, and have the Baltimore Catechism memorized backward and forward.

Cecilia resigned herself to the noise and general chaos and took as her mission statement a paraphrase of Father John Hardon, S.J.: "If you live your faith, your children will learn their catechism." As she carried the kids or the laundry—or both—up the stairs, she'd pause before her favorite crucifix and say, "I'm doing this for you."

Sometimes she'd get a bit overwhelmed with it all and would lock her kids out in the yard. Sister Chiara laughs about a time when she got herself stuck in a tree and called "Mom!" for what seemed like hours. Finally her mom came out, looked up in the tree, and said, "You got yourself up there. You get yourself down." She wanted the kids to think twice about getting themselves into potentially bad situations and to resolve things themselves if possible.

Yet, she was always there when they needed her. And like all good parents, she and Bill were also there when the kids didn't want them to be. Not the two nun-wannabes, surely? With daughters, the issue is always clothes. "The low-rise jeans with the belly showing? Genevieve and Regina put us through that," Cecilia says. "We were adamant that there be no skin showing."

Kids may complain about boundaries, but they need them to feel secure. With nine kids in the family, boundaries have a way of setting themselves. One was that the kids could not have everything they wanted. They had to work for it.

"Genevieve and I begged for American Girl dolls," Sister Chiara says. In response, Cecilia pointed to a collection of naked dolls with knotted hair, lying in the bottom of the closet. Two hundred bucks for two more dolls? Not happening. So the girls went around the neighborhood taking orders from the neighbors for cookies. They baked them and delivered them. They made seventy-five dollars. Although they were short on cash, no one can deny that they were loaded with work ethic. Mom and Dad rewarded their industry. "In the end," Sister Chiara says, "Santa brought the dolls and we spent the money on their accessories."

Like other kids, the Cunningham kids sometimes resented having to wait for what they got. Sister Chiara says, "I asked for something at the thrift store once, but Mom had her hands full and she was just leaving, and she just didn't have time to bother with it." She confesses that at the time she thought, "But I never ask for things, and besides I'm so sweet tempered!" But now she is grateful for those moments of waiting and self-denial. They helped her fight her innate sense of wounded pride.

As one of the older kids, she was also expected to help her busy mom care for her younger siblings. This was purgative also. She may be a nun now, but she was no angel. Do angels grumble under their breath because they wake up groggy and have to get breakfast on the table for their younger siblings? The oldest kids fed their younger siblings, bathed them, helped them with their homework, read to them, and played with them. Joseph, Genevieve, and Regina used to tell their younger siblings, "We've done everything but give birth to you!"

Helping with the little kids was inconvenient much of the time. But is inconvenience always a bad thing? We must all stand in line; we all have to yield in traffic. Growing up with little kids bugging you gives you practice.

But little kids are not always a bother. Bathing them, reading to them, and playing with them can be fun. It's the kind of stuff that bonds siblings together.

This is good because kids who live in close quarters had better learn to get along. The Cunninghams were doubled, tripled, and sometimes quadrupled in their rooms. For a while, Joseph slept on a mattress pulled out from under a bed. To the world, this is a clear argument against having so many children.

Yet, in the midst of their sacrifices, the Cunninghams felt they had much to share. So as soon as they were old enough, the kids started volunteering. Genevieve and Regina volunteered for three years at a therapeutic riding school. They earned some riding lessons from the deal. Regina also built homes for the poor in the Appalachians.

The gutsiest thing Regina did was take part in a chastity-outreach program at the beach. She and another girl handed out pamphlets and tried to tell strangers that they were worthy of respect. They got all kinds of reactions: positive, indifferent, and negative. It was all worth it for the one young girl who cried.

At eighteen, Regina entered Our Lady of the Angels Monastery in Hanceville, Alabama. She is one of the Poor Clares of Perpetual Adoration. This is Mother Angelica's outfit. Genevieve went to college first and then entered the same monastery at the age of twenty-one.

The world does not understand why anyone, let alone a lovely young person, would embrace a celibate life. "What a waste." And the world is right. The world, without realizing it, has stumbled onto the very essence of religious life: a complete giving up of the best of oneself for God.

In the Old Testament, the faithful sacrificed the best of their flocks and herds to be slain and burnt. This was their way of totally honoring God, who had given them everything. In the New Testament, God outdid them by sacrificing his best—his Son. The people of the world looked on, shaking their heads. They didn't understand it then. They don't understand it now. "Come down from that cross and we will believe you."

People might wonder if Bill and Cecilia pushed the girls to become nuns, the way people sometimes push their kids to become doctors or lawyers. Bill and Cecilia take neither blame nor credit. "The call comes from God. We have no idea how it got lodged in their hearts."

Sister Chiara says that, yes, the call is from God, but there is more to it than that. She knows herself. Under different circumstances, it could have all gone very differently. "I would never have found my true vocation if it weren't for my parents."

Saying Yes to Patience

Bill and Cecilia believed that in spite of the generations of sorrow in their backgrounds, their children could be the first of many generations to be happy. They saw their role as "the humble excavating and cinderblock work."

Setting a firm foundation is all any of us parents are called to do. Mother Janet Erskine Stuart, in writing to her teaching sisters in *The Education of Catholic Girls*, says that those who have charge over the young should strive to begin a great work rather than to finish a small one. I imagine it as laying the foundations of a great cathedral. Picture the workers, their eyes ever pointed at the ground, their backs bent, their hands roughened with labor. For what? No one beholding a great cathedral does more than glance at its substructure. People look up, up, at the prismatic light filtered through the rose window, streaming through the airy open space, playing off the lofty vaulted ceilings, coming to rest upon the living stone reliefs of the Virgin and Child. Yet, none of it would stand without that humble, firm foundation.

Somehow we've been conditioned to expect more immediate rewards from a life of grace. We want salvation to come in an altar call, dramatic and instantaneous. The humble foundation work is not glorious, but it is solid. Similarly, grace is passed on simply, from one person to another—from a little boy who picked up his brother in church and kissed him, to a little girl destined to be a mother, to a young teen standing on the beach, to another who, moments before, was broken and weeping.

Epilogue

It is the mark of all good Catholics to think they are bad Catholics. It is no wonder, then, the parents I talked to for this book think it a miracle that God gave them such exceptional children.

Their children know better.

God does not often do miracles. He uses human wills, human choices, and even human failings to accomplish his great work.

So do not think that it is beyond you to raise extraordinary children like the parents you have just read about. Instead, take confidence in their success. The more ordinary you are, the more glory there is for God.

You may never see the results of your labors. Or if you do, they may appear small—mere drops in an otherwise dried-up river. Be faithful.

One child who grew up faithful became a solitary seminarian who by the laying on of hands became another Christ. That young man inspired this mother to seek out others like him and to pass on their example to other parents. And so the drops gather in the hope that our small efforts in our homes will please God who will make the Church flow once more with vitality. Perhaps that seminary will even reopen, and the long grand corridor will be filled, once again, with the sounds of life.

Acknowledgments

Thank you to all the priests, sisters, and nuns, and to your families, for allowing all of us into your homes. It was worth the visit.

Thanks to Ave Maria Press for seeking me out and for letting me write my own, quirky version of a parenting book.

Thank you to everyone who asked me to write another humor book. I hope this counts.

Thanks to my husband, Greg, for his unflagging zeal for my writing and for being the manly half of this parenting adventure and to our kids for thinking my stories about them are hilarious.

Thank you to the busy people who took time to read and comment on excerpts of this work: Dessi Jackson, Daria Sockey, the faithful Dan Sheehan, and the ever encouraging Elizabeth Douglas. Your free books are on the way.

Special thanks to Duncan Anderson (and Karen and the kids) for staying up nights to help me sort the rough from the smooth.

And to Art and Laraine Bennett for saying "Yes!"

Susie Lloyd is the award-winning author of two humor books: *Please Don't Drink the Holy Water* and *Bless Me, Father, for I Have Kids*. Her work has appeared in *Catholic Digest, National Catholic Register, Crisis, Franciscan Way, and The Latin Mass*. She is a graduate of Thomas More College of Liberal Arts in New Hampshire, which prepared her for life as a career homeschooler. She and her husband Greg have six daughters, one son, and one son-in-law. Lloyd does much of her writing from her office on wheels: the middle bench of her beat-up Suburban. She and her family live in Pennsylvania.

Founded in 1865, Ave Maria Press,
a ministry of the Congregation of
Holy Cross, is a Catholic publishing
company that serves the spiritual and
formative needs of the Church and its
schools, institutions, and ministers;
Christian individuals and families; and
others seeking spiritual nourishment.

For a complete listing of titles from

Ave Maria Press

Sorin Books

Forest of Peace

Christian Classics

visit www.avemariapress.com

ave maria press® / Notre Dame, IN 46556
A Ministry of the United States Province of Holy Cross